Nahum, Habakkuk, Zephaniah, and Haggai

BIBLE STUDY COMMENTARY

Nahum, Habakkuk, Zephaniah, and Haggai

J. N. Boo Heflin

Lamplighter Books Grand Rapids, Michigan
Zondervan Publishing House

NAHUM, HABAKKUK, ZEPHANIAH, AND HAGGAI:
BIBLE STUDY COMMENTARY
Copyright © 1985 by The Zondervan Corporation
Grand Rapids, Michigan

Lamplighter Books is an imprint of Zondervan Publishing House,
1415 Lake Drive, S.E., Grand Rapids, Michigan 49506.

Library of Congress Cataloging in Publication Data

Heflin, J. N. Boo.
 Nahum, Habakkuk, Zephaniah, and Haggai.

 (Bible study commentary series)
 Bibliography: p:
 1. Bible. O.T. Minor Prophets—Commentaries. I. Title. II Series.
BS1560.H42 1985   224'.907   85-26321
ISBN 0-310-27531-8

Edited by Janet Kobobel

Printed in the United States of America

86 87 88 89 90 91 / 10 9 8 7 6 5 4 3 2 1

To Mary,
with whom I am learning
the meaning of Genesis 2:18–25

Contents

Acknowledgments

Many people have contributed in some way to this commentary, not the least are my many teachers over the years. Some have taught me in the classroom; others have been my mentors through their writings. They have all played a significant role in this book. I especially wish to thank Stan Gundry of Zondervan Publishing House for giving me the privilege of participating in this series.

Likewise, Janet Kobobel of Zondervan deserves special commendation for her valuable assistance, encouragement, and friendship.

In a special way I am indebted to the administration and staff of Southwestern Seminary for assistance at so many points. I owe a debt of gratitude to Dr. Bill Tolar, Mrs. Jean Bell, and the staff of Roberts Library, whose helpfulness in many ways will not be forgotten. Ruth Ann Foster, my secretary and graduate assistant, and Donna Smith, wife of my colleague Ebbie, spent long hours typing the first and final drafts of the manuscript; they also offered many helpful suggestions. I am grateful for their major contribution to this work.

I give a special word of thanks to my three children—Judy, Sherry, and David. Though they did not read the manuscript or make writing suggestions, they gave of themselves. On many occasions, they forfeited time with their dad so he could write; they did so without complaint. I profoundly appreciate them.

Finally I thank Mary, my wife and best friend, without whose love, support, encouragement, assistance, and patience this project would never have been completed.

Preface

Two major eras in Judah's history constitute the time frame of the four prophets examined in this commentary: the years just before the Babylonian exile (630–587 B.C.) and the years immediately after the exile (539–520 B.C.). Nahum, Zephaniah, and Habakkuk were among the prophets of the former period. Haggai was the first prophetic figure in the post-exilic era.

I wrote this commentary to be used with an open Bible. When you come to the discussion of a section of Scripture, read the biblical text as a unit first; then read the commentary remarks, referring to the Scripture. While the commentary could be read straight through, to isolate it from the Scripture is to miss its explanatory and supplementary purposes. Follow this simple formula for the greatest benefit: Bible first, then commentary with Bible.

Translations of the Hebrew and Septuagint texts and other possible readings are my own, unless otherwise indicated. With rare exceptions, quotations from a standard translation are from the *New International Version*. Three abbreviations used in this commentary are: NIV (*New International Version*), LXX (the Greek Septuagint), and KJV (*King James Version*).

> Boo Heflin
> Southwestern Baptist Theological Seminary
> Fort Worth, Texas

Chapter 1

An Introduction to Nahum and His Prophecy

Each prophetic book raises its own set of questions which lead commentators to widely divergent answers. The Book of Nahum, with its single theme of the destruction of Nineveh, is no exception. Some scholars even question Nahum's prophetic status, concluding that he was a false prophet at best. Others, while affirming the book's literary merit, conclude that Nahum contains little, if any, devotional, theological, or ethical value for the modern reader.

Such critical disparagement is unwarranted. Nothing in Nahum's work removes him from the mainstream of the Old Testament prophetic movement. In his forty-seven short verses he concentrates on *one* major issue. Needless to say, he makes no comment on many issues of ancient Israel's faith. What is said, however, is potent biblical theology of great value to any and every age.

A. Nahum the Man

Of Nahum the prophet little is known. No mention is made of him outside this book that bears his name, and information in the book is extremely limited. Such factors as his date of birth, his parentage and family, the site of his preaching, his occupation, the experience of his call, and his death are all missing from the three chapters. Some of these matters are open to "a reasoned speculation," but, for the most part, they are beyond recovery. Despite the obvious difficulty, a close examination of the book reveals at least a sketch of the man.

1. Nahum's Name

Names were very important in the Old Testament world, often revealing something of the bearer's character, background, nature, or task. In the prophets' case, names often revealed the theme of their preaching.

The name "Nahum" occurs only once in his book (1:1) and nowhere else in the Old Testament; mention of another Nahum is made in Joseph's genealogy in Luke 3:25. Although the name Nahum was not frequently used in the Bible, it may have been a common name. Archaeologists have found numerous potsherds from ancient Palestine bearing the inscription "of Nahum, son of Abdi," perhaps referring to a hereditary family of potters. The name also has been found on ancient Phoenician inscriptions. Likewise it may be related to a number of other names found in the Hebrew Bible, including Naham (1 Chron. 4:19), Nahamani (Neh. 7:7), Menahem (2 Kings 15:14), Tanhumeth (Jer. 40:8), and Nehemiah.

Commentators suggest various translations for Nahum, including: "comfort," "comforter," "consoling," "consoler," "compassion," and "relief." A comparison with words of similar form has led some scholars to translate the name as "full of comfort." Some believe it is an abbreviated form of the word "Nahum-yah" and thus means "Yahweh gives comfort" or "Yahweh is comfort" or "the comfort of Yahweh" or "Yahweh is full of comfort."

Most scholars see the prophet's name representing a positive message for the book. That is, in light of Nahum's preaching, Judah will know comfort. Its comfort comes because God is about to act in history against Judah's oppressor, wicked Nineveh.

But is it possible that the name represents a *negative* message? The only other occurrence in the book of the basic Hebrew verbal form from which the name Nahum comes is in 3:7.[1] This verse contains a totally negative word to Nineveh; the prophet declares, "Where can I find anyone to comfort you?" Perhaps the prophet's name is meant to convey the message that there is *no comfort* for Nineveh.

---

[1] Hebrew nouns often come from verb roots. Such is the case with the name "Nahum," which comes from a Hebrew verb meaning "to comfort, console."

2. Nahum's Family

While detailed information is available about the families of many prophetic figures, nothing is known about Nahum's family. Jerome, the great biblical scholar of the early church, in the preface to his commentary on Nahum, indicates that a number of ancient writers interpreted the phrase "the Elkoshite" in 1:1 to designate Nahum's father. The name was read as either "Elcesaeus" or "Helkeseus." Jerome also said that Hebrew tradition considered this man to be a prophet, just as his son was. Today no one accepts this ancient view. Scholars now recognize that the word "Elkoshite" refers to Nahum's home rather than to his parentage.

3. Nahum's Home

The reference to "the Elkoshite" is the only mention in the entire Bible of the place called Elkosh. Scholars have not been able to locate the whereabouts of this ancient town, but various traditions suggest three major Middle Eastern sections for its location: Assyria, Galilee (the territory of the northern kingdom of Israel), and Judah (the southern kingdom).

The Assyrian site identified as Elkosh is a city on the eastern side of the Tigris River. Today the city is called Al-Qush (notice the similarity in the consonants of the two names). It is located twenty-five miles north of the present-day city of Mosul in Iraq.[2] A local tradition suggests that Nahum's tomb is located there.

Those who feel that Al-Qush is Nahum's Elkosh believe that the prophet was descended from Israelites of the northern kingdom who were deported to Mesopotamia after the fall of Samaria in 722 B.C. They contend that Nahum's intimate knowledge of Nineveh demands that he actually lived in the vicinity of the great city.

Most contemporary commentators, however, reject the Assyrian site for ancient Elkosh and rightly so. Research indicates that no ancient writer ever identified Al-Qush as Elkosh. In fact, the first mention of Al-Qush does not appear

---

[2] The ruins of ancient Nineveh are on the eastern side of the Tigris River, directly across from Mosul.

until the eighth century A.D. Furthermore, the tradition that
Nahum's tomb is in Al-Qush cannot be dated further back than
the sixteenth century A.D.[3] Also note that Nahum's knowledge of
Nineveh was what one would expect from an intelligent
Hebrew citizen of that day, regardless of where he lived.
Two sites in Galilee have been identified as possibly being
the ancient Elkosh.[4] One is a place called Helkesei or Elkese.
This location is a little more credible than Al-Qush because the
tradition associating it with Nahum is much earlier. Jerome
reported that in his day Helkesei had an established reputation
as Nahum's city.

A second Galilean site suggested for Elkosh is Capernaum,
which means "the village of Nahum." Yet there is absolutely no
evidence that Capernaum was ever known as Elkosh. Also there
is no proof that the city is named after the prophet Nahum.

While it seems more likely that Nahum came from Galilee
rather than Assyria, the Galilean sites for Elkosh are likewise
highly questionable. In fact, by the late seventh century B.C.,
when Nahum probably lived, Galilee had little significance to
the Old Testament story because it was the territory of the old
northern kingdom destroyed by Assyria in 722 B.C.

The Judean location for Elkosh is probably best. Judah is
certainly the setting for the Old Testament story after 722 B.C.
Also Nahum emphasizes the southern kingdom in his preaching
(see 1:15). However, an exact location for Elkosh in Judean
territory has not been determined, though scholars have suggested ancient Eleutheropolis, as well as Kessijeh, Umm Lagish,
and Bir el Kaus.

---

[3] An older tradition describes a Mesopotamian burial place for Nahum. In 1165
A.D., a Benjamin of Tudela reported that he had seen Nahum's tomb at Ain
Japhata, south of Babylon. Obviously these traditions are of little historical
significance.

[4] Some commentators have appealed to John 7:52 to argue against a Galilean
origin for Nahum. That verse says in part: ". . . you will find that a prophet does
not come out of Galilee." Note, however, that Jonah came from Gath-hepher, a
Galilean town in Zebulon (see Jonah 1:1; 2 Kings 14:25). Though scholars
debate the issue, it seems certain that the passage in John has some meaning
related more to the New Testament historical context than to the larger history of
Israel.

4. Nahum's Date

Old Testament prophetic books often include notices of the place or time of writing in their titles. Nahum's title in 1:1 has neither. Thus scholars have fervently debated the date of Nahum's ministry.

The ancient Jewish historian Josephus placed Nahum in the reign of Judah's King Jotham, while Clement of Alexandria put him between Daniel and Ezekiel. Most commentators in the nineteenth century, following the lead of Jerome, assigned Nahum to Hezekiah's reign, making him a contemporary of Isaiah and Micah.

The archaeological discovery of Nineveh in the mid-nineteenth century and the subsequent discovery of the Assyrian King Asshurbanapal's library gave commentators valuable information from which to interpret a pivotal section in Nahum. Thus they established the *terminus a quo* (starting point) for the book's writing. Reference is made in 3:8–10 to the Egyptian city of Thebes and its downfall. For years scholars had discounted the historical significance of this passage because there was no established evidence for such a defeat of this city. Asshurbanapal's library, however, revealed the sack of Thebes by that Assyrian monarch. The date of this event has been placed at 663 B.C. The prophet's mention of the sack of the Egyptian city as an illustration of what will happen to Nineveh proves that he wrote *after* that event.

Since Nahum is predicting Nineveh's fall, the *terminus ad quem* (ending) for the book is 612 B.C., the year the great Assyrian city was destroyed. Nineveh was crushed in August of that year by the Babylonians and their allies.

Knowledge of these two historical events leads to the conclusion that Nahum wrote sometime between the years 663 and 612 B.C.[5] Some commentators point out that the event in

---

[5] Some scholars believe the book was written *after* Nineveh's fall; their interpretations vary greatly. Paul Humbert, for example, concluded that the writing took place very soon after Nineveh's defeat and that the book was used as a liturgy to celebrate the hated enemy's fall. Other positions are even more radical. Paul Riessler argued that the Nineveh of Nahum is not the Assyrian capital but an obscure town in northern Mesopotamia; its fall came in the late exilic period. Paul Haupt and Otto Happel contended that the book was written in the Maccabean period. Happel interpreted Nineveh to be an eschatological symbol for the enemies of God rather than the Assyrian city.

3:8–10 seems fresh on the prophet's mind and thus conclude that the book was written closer to the 663 B.C. date. On the other hand, the majority of scholars today, feeling that Nahum's words are almost an eyewitness account of Nineveh's fall, date the book closer to 612 B.C.

While it is difficult to be more precise than the general period of 663 to 612 B.C., Nahum contains some internal clues that may help. For example, 1:12 leaves the impression that Nineveh was strong and its power unchecked when the prophet wrote. If that is so, it would suggest moving the date of writing to a period prior to 626 B.C. Before 626 B.C. Assyria, though beginning to show signs of internal weakness, was still quite strong. After the death of the powerful Asshurbanapal in 627 B.C. and the Babylonian revolt around 626 B.C., the nation began to crumble. From 625 to 609 B.C., the situation for Assyria went downhill in a hurry. The fall of the old capital Asshur came in 614 B.C., the fall of Nineveh in 612 B.C., and the total and final defeat of Assyrian forces in 609 B.C. Thus in the period after 626 B.C., Nineveh does not seem to be the awesome city reflected in 1:12.

Likewise, 1:13 seems to indicate that Judah was still in the grip of Assyrian domination at the time of the prophet's writing. This interpretation would also push back the date of Nahum to before Assyria's collapse, that is, to 626 B.C. or before. Judah was free from the Assyrian yoke after this date.

In light of these internal clues, it seems best to date the writing of Nahum sometime between the years 663 and 626 B.C. To narrow the issue down more is impossible until further evidence is uncovered. If Nahum is placed in the later years of that time frame, he was a contemporary of Jeremiah (who was called to his ministry in 626 B.C.) and Zephaniah.

5. Nahum's Personality

A character sketch of Nahum is difficult, considering both the paucity of information about him in the Bible and the brevity of his book. There is certainly no legitimate way to psychoanalyze the man from such a distance in time. Nevertheless, some of his characteristics are evident.

First, Nahum was an accomplished poet. Most commentators underscore his literary gift. He wrote with a sense of the dramatic, using vivid, striking, and highly descriptive imagery. As was true with other prophetic figures, Nahum used a variety of literary devices to get across his message.[6] It is not an overstatement to conclude that his literary craftsmanship is unexcelled in the Old Testament.

Second, Nahum was an ardent patriot. His deep love for Judah is seen in the hostility he has for the nation's great enemy, Nineveh. He exhibits almost a sense of exaltation as he announces the prophetic woes of judgment against "the city of blood" (3:1). Some commentators even see him expressing a malicious joy at Nineveh's overthrow, a gloating hatred toward this ancient enemy.

But in affirming Nahum's patriotism, is it valid to brand him as a nationalist? The nationalist lives by the creed "my country, right or wrong." The true Old Testament prophet would never affirm such a philosophy. He would say "my country" and say it with pride, love, and deepest affection. But he would also declare, "My country, be it right according to the will of God."

In his strong words against Nineveh, is Nahum overlooking the sins of his own people? Many commentators accuse him of just that. But their negative assessment is not necessarily the definitive word. One should first remember that Nahum's single theme is Nineveh's fall. The prophet simply is not dealing with Judah. And yet, in a pointed word to his people in 1:15 (2:1 in Hebrew), he calls them to celebrate their festivals and to fulfill their vows.[7] The prophet is emphasizing the necessity of Judah's positive relationship with God (the very brevity of this verse makes it stand out as significant in the total message of the book).

In conjunction with the implication of this verse, consider the clear message of Nahum that Nineveh will be judged not because it is Judah's enemy, but because it is God's enemy. Anyone who flaunts self in proud rebellion against God—Judah as well as Nineveh—will eventually face divine judgment.

---

[6] For example, Nahum used repetition in 1:2; metaphors and similes in 1:10, 2:7, 2:12, 3:4, 3:12, 3:17; graphic illustration in 3:8-10; and rhetorical questions in 1:6, 1:9, 2:11, 3:7, 3:8, and 3:19.

[7] Some commentators would see in these instructions little more than an emphasis on external religious practice.

Nahum was not among the false, nationalistic prophets of that day like Hananiah (Jer. 28) who told the people all was well when it was not. Nahum was a patriot who strongly loved his own nation and obviously wanted his people to be rightly related to God. His message was that Nineveh would fall because of the city's rebellion against God (1:9, 11). That must be a lesson to all others, including Judah. Surely the prophet who believed in divine judgment for human rebellion and shared it with his people loved his country more than the one who failed to call the people to the priority of a relationship with God.

Third, Nahum was a man with an abiding faith in God. As a Judean citizen of the seventh century B.C., he had lived all of his years under the oppressive hand of the Assyrians. He had witnessed the cruelty and ruthlessness that had brought humiliation and agony to his people. He had seen their obvious and flagrant rebellion against God (1:9).

Yet deeply embedded within the prophet was the overwhelming belief that evil could not stand forever. Trusting in divine justice as well as divine goodness, Nahum finally stood to proclaim the Lord's message: "Assyria will be no more!" His faith was so real, his conviction so genuine, that his message reads as if it is the eyewitness account of one who stood in Nineveh in 612 B.C. and literally saw the great city fall. Actually, as considered earlier, his message was probably delivered several years before the event. Nahum was able to see with the eye of a living and vibrant faith in God.

Fourth, Nahum was a man of righteous indignation. Sensitive by nature, he was incensed by Assyria's inhumanity to people. While his contemporary, Jeremiah, often agonized over the perplexing problem of the wicked's prosperity,[8] Nahum unequivocally and without apology proclaimed the reality of God's judgment on the wicked.[9]

---

[8] See, for example, Jeremiah 12:1. This comment is not meant in any way to demean Jeremiah, who also declared God's judgment without apology (see Jer. 7:1–8:3), but rather to show Nahum's single-mindedness.

[9] For an excellent discussion of the necessity for righteous indignation, see Raymond Calkins's *The Modern Message of the Minor Prophets* (New York and London: Harper & Brothers, 1947), pp. 83–87. Calkins concludes that everyone who loves God must on occasion prophesy like Nahum.

B. Nahum the Book

The Book of Nahum is the seventh in the collection of Old Testament books known as the twelve minor prophets. It follows Micah in the Hebrew Bible, the Latin Vulgate, and the modern versions. While still the seventh book, it follows Jonah in the LXX.

1. The Purpose of the Book of Nahum

While the theme of Nahum is Nineveh's fall, what was the purpose of this message? Some commentators say the prophet spoke directly and solely to Nineveh itself. His purpose was to declare that the city's destruction would soon be realized.

Others feel Nahum's purpose was to comfort Judah. After years of Assyrian persecution, what better word was there for his people than that the end of the hated enemy was in sight?

Both of these positions, especially the second, may contain some truth. But perhaps the real key to understanding the purpose of Nahum is to recognize the theological foundation in his proclamation. The Book of Nahum affirms the theological truth that wickedness can go only so far in the presence of the righteous God. Judgment against human rebellion is a reality in a world under divine sovereignty. It is the purpose of Nahum to proclaim that truth, both for his day and for every other day.

2. The Nature of the Literature in Nahum

The Book of Nahum is poetry. One of the earliest scholars to recognize its poetic character was E. J. Greve in 1793. Since that time commentators have generally agreed with the assessment. Nahum has often been favorably compared with other major Hebrew poems like the Song of Deborah in Judges 5 and David's lament over Saul and Jonathan in 2 Samuel 1:17–27.

Parallelism (the main feature in Hebrew poetry), colorful language, peculiar syntax,[10] and several examples of the Qinah measure are present in Nahum. The Qinah measure, which is a lament or dirge style, is characterized by a verse with two lines, in which the first is at least one accent longer than the second.

---

[10] One characteristic of Hebrew poetry is such peculiar syntax as the absence of relatives, particles, and articles. In Nahum the definite article is used only fourteen times.

As one reads the Qinah measure, the imbalance in the lines suggests that the speaker's voice has broken or cracked. The effect, which unfortunately is often lost in translation, seems to capture the intense emotion expressed by the writer.[11]

While the Book of Nahum definitely reflects a poetic style, the meter is not easily determined. Commentators differ widely in their conclusions about the prophet's metrical patterns. In their efforts to demonstrate meter in the book, some scholars have taken great liberty with the text. They have transposed verses, omitted words and even sections of verses, added words and phrases, as well as radically changed the received text. For the most part, this alteration has been done with absolutely no manuscript support. The net result is to rob Nahum's work of its intensity and prophetic intent.

Perhaps the difficulty in locating specific metrical patterns comes because some scholars want to find what is not there. Nahum's concern was not to shape and form regular poetic devices but rather to proclaim God's Word. The key for the prophet was not in the form but in the message. Totally inspired, stirred by the historical situation and his abiding faith in God, Nahum allowed his imagination free rein. The result is the magnificent yet terrifying portrayal of Nineveh's judgment at the hand of the sovereign God. The poetic meter of the prophet's proclamation is, therefore, irregular and not subject to precise identification.

Not only is the Book of Nahum poetic literature, but it is also prophetic literature. Its place in the canon assures its acceptance as prophecy. Present in the book is evidence of the prophetic tasks of both foretelling and forthtelling.[12] Elements often found in the writings of the Old Testament prophets make their appearance in Nahum. These elements include the vision (2:3–10), the oracle of judgment (2:13), the prophetic woe (3:1), the taunt song (3:8–10), and the dirge (3:18–19).

---

[11] The Qinah measure is found in the Hebrew text of Nahum 1:11, 2:11–12, 3:4, 3:18, and elsewhere.

[12] As a foreteller, the prophet predicted. Nahum fulfilled this role in the specific prediction that Nineveh would fall. As a forthteller, the prophet acted as God's representative who spoke directly to the needs of the people of his own day. Nahum's role at this point was to demonstrate that Nineveh's fall came for theological reasons (its rejection of God and worship of idols) and was an object lesson for all, even Judah.

3. Critical Problems in the Book of Nahum

Scholars do not agree about the quality of the Hebrew text of Nahum. Conservative scholars generally recognize it to be in reasonably good condition, whereas others find a great deal of corruption. One's perception of problems regarding the Hebrew text is often lessened or heightened by the position taken on other critical issues in the book. Three such issues are: (1) the possibility of an alphabetical acrostic arrangement, (2) the unity of the book, and (3) the liturgical use of the book.

In his commentary on the Psalms in 1894, Franz Delitzsch cited the earlier suggestions of Frohnmeyer, a pastor from Württemberg, that there were traces of an acrostic in Nahum 1. Since then Old Testament scholars have devoted many hours trying to reconstruct the acrostic but with little success.

Acrostics are common in the Old Testament. Psalm 119 is perhaps the best-known, while other examples can be found in Psalms 9, 10, 25, 34, 111, 145. This literary device was used as an aid for memorization of the material.

While many commentators conclude there is a Nahum acrostic, they have not been able to agree about its limits. Those who see the acrostic in the first chapter identify Nahum 1:2 as its beginning. There the *aleph,* the first letter of the Hebrew alphabet, is used for the first word of the line. The search for the other letters continues from that point. The acrostic is taken only to verses 8, 9, or 10 by most scholars; this section supposedly contains anywhere from eleven to sixteen letters of the alphabet. A few commentators take the acrostic all the way to Nahum 2:3 or 2:4 and see it encompassing the entire twenty-two letter alphabet.

The lack of agreement on the number of Hebrew letters used leads to the question: What was the original structure of the acrostic? Some commentators conclude the acrostic never contained more than half of the alphabet. Others feel it originally contained the whole alphabet but much has been confused, rearranged, and corrupted through transmission. It has even been suggested that part of the acrostic was lost when a scribe ran out of room on a scroll!

Efforts to locate the missing letters have led commentators

to redesign the text radically to fit the acrostic pattern. The order of verses has been rearranged, and words have even been moved around within verses—all to fit a scheme. But despite the assumption that the acrostic is there, its presence has not been demonstrated with any assurance. It is quite unlikely that it will ever be reconstructed with certainty—if it exists at all.

A second critical issue in the study of Nahum is the book's unity. For centuries Nahum was generally regarded as a literary unit written by the prophet from Elkosh. In 1814 a scholar named Berthold suggested that the three chapters, while all from the hand of Nahum, were independent of each other and were composed at different times in his ministry. With the exception of some scholars who questioned the genuineness of the title in Nahum 1:1, the matter was left there until the end of the nineteenth century. In 1893 Hermann Gunkel took the issue further, questioning Nahum's authorship of portions of the book.

One factor that led Gunkel and then others to this conclusion was the supposed existence of the acrostic. Some commentators asserted that this poem was older than the Book of Nahum. The prophet himself, they reasoned, incorporated the acrostic into his work to serve as the theological introduction for the prophecy. Most, however, contended the acrostic was much later than Nahum's book and was appended to the prophecy in the third or even second century B.C.[13]

Arguments for non-Nahumic authorship of the acrostic are highly subjective. The following are representative: (1) The literary quality of the first chapter of Nahum is decidedly inferior to chapters 2 and 3. With its acrostic structure, it is much too artificial and mechanical for the prophet's vigorous proclamation. (2) The Hebrew text of the acrostic is much more corrupt than the remainder of the book. (3) The first chapter makes no reference to Nineveh (which was, of course, Nahum's subject). The descriptions are so general they could apply to anyone. (4) The first chapter has a didactic purpose, that is, it is designed to explain the lesson underlying the message of

---

[13] Some advocates of this position conclude that Nahum's first original word does not come until Nahum 1:11. Since that verse seems an unlikely beginning for the prophet's message, they further conclude that some of the original message was removed to make room for the acrostic.

Nineveh's fall. Such a purpose, according to those who hold the view of non-Nahumic authorship of chapter 1, comes from the post-exilic age of reflection rather than from the period of the active prophets. In other words, these commentators contend that Nahum's only task was to announce Nineveh's fall; to give any meaning to the event was beyond his concern.

Though the acrostic was the original issue in the discussion of the book's unity, other passages soon became subject to close scrutiny. It is safe to say today that no verse in the Book of Nahum has escaped the conclusion by someone that it is not written by Nahum. Some of the commentaries recognize no more than a third of the book as Nahum's writing.

No valid reason exists, however, for not accepting Nahum's authorship of the entire book. The arguments mentioned above for non-Nahumic authorship of the acrostic lend themselves to different interpretations. For example, the position that Nahum 1 is inferior literature is purely and simply a value judgment. Furthermore, both of the first two arguments fall when one recognizes that the so-called acrostic has never been demonstrated with assurance.

The argument that chapter 1 makes no reference to Nineveh ignores the title in Nahum 1:1. Then it ignores the simple truth that Nahum, in the initial verses of his message, is formulating his theological foundation. It seems quite appropriate that Nineveh is *not* mentioned here. The theological truth undergirding the prophet's announcement of Nineveh's fall can be applied to anyone.

The final argument, to say that the prophets simply announced events without regard to their meaning, is to deny the purpose of Old Testament prophetic literature. Over and over again the Old Testament prophet interprets God's activity to the people. If there were no didactic purposes in the prophetic messages, they would have little relevance for any age, including their own.

There are valid arguments for affirming Nahum's authorship. Manuscript evidence, for example, overwhelmingly presents the book as a literary unit. Likewise, a reading of Nahum as found in the received text is clear, vivid, and understandable. The arbitrary emendations by scholars often cause more difficulties for comprehension than the text does as it stands.

A third critical issue in the study of Nahum concerns the liturgical use of the book. This novel approach to Nahum comes from a small band of commentators in this century. They contend that Nahum is not a prophecy but a liturgy written for worship in the temple. The book, according to this view, was written *after* Nineveh's fall.

The earliest supporter of this view evidently was Paul Haupt. In 1907 he asserted that the book is a liturgy of four separate poems. Haupt believed these poems were composed for a Jewish celebration of victory over the Syrians in 161 B.C.

A more highly developed liturgical approach came from Paul Humbert in the period from 1926 to 1932. Ernst Sellin and Friedrich Horst, among others, support his theory. Humbert believed the liturgy was written immediately after Nineveh's fall in 612 B.C. to be used in a Jewish New Year festival that autumn.

Humbert found a clue for his position in the questions in Nahum. They represented for him a liturgical character. Thus he tried to show in Nahum complicated antiphonal sections in which worship leaders would ask questions and worshipers would give responsive answers. Humbert's theory demands radical alteration of the Hebrew text in a number of places to demonstrate an antiphonal pattern.

The liturgical approach has not gained much sympathy from the majority of commentators. Perhaps portions of Nahum were used at times in temple worship, but that in no way disqualifies the book as a work of genuine prophecy.

4. Influences on the Writing of Nahum

Environment plays a major role in determining character. This does not mean that we are simply victims of our environment; surely the Bible underscores a person's freedom to make life-changing decisions. Nonetheless, one's home, the major people in one's life, and the significant events experienced all help to form and shape the person.

Nahum too was a part of his environment. If more of his background were known, he could be better understood. His book, however, does reveal at least two influences on his life and message.

First, it seems quite likely that Nahum was influenced by the earlier writings of Isaiah. Various words and phrases in Nahum appear to be echoes from Isaiah.[14]

It is not surprising that parallels can be found. The prophets were familiar with their predecessors. Furthermore, the prophets shared a common theological tradition which would also account for points of similarity in their presentations.

Second, Nahum was influenced by Nineveh's barbarous reign. Perhaps the most notorious butchers of the ancient world, the Assyrians were guilty of unspeakable horrors.[15] Nahum had seen these things firsthand. With each passing day, his anger had grown. He was outraged at the deepest level of his being.

But Nahum's anger was not on a personal level, nor even on a national and political level. He was not aroused simply because of wrong done by the Assyrians to himself or to his people or to other peoples. For Nahum, Nineveh's wrong was against God Himself. He saw in Nineveh a personification of evil and sin. As a devout worshiper of the righteous God, Nahum had to take sin seriously. For the prophet, the ruthlessness practiced by Nineveh was evidence of the cosmic struggle between right and wrong, good and evil, righteousness and sin. Thus it was out of the growing outrage over the reality of evil itself that Nahum passionately called for Nineveh's end. A terrible price will always be paid for sin.

5. *Major Theological Themes in the Book of Nahum*

Modern commentators generally offer Nahum little praise. His theology is said to be deficient at best. But as the preceding discussion emphasizes, Nahum's message grew out of genuine theological concerns. He was no zealous nationalist, gleefully

---

[14] For examples of the relationship of the two books, compare Nahum 1:13 with Isaiah 10:27 and Nahum 3:10 with Isaiah 13:16. Another obvious parallel is Nahum 1:15 and Isaiah 52:7. Many scholars, however, think the Isaiah 52 passage comes from a later Isaianic prophet in the exilic period; if so, he was influenced by Nahum.

[15] Their cruelties included pouring boiling tar on victims' heads, gouging out eyes, tearing out tongues, skinning people alive and then covering pillars and city walls with the skins, cutting off female prisoners' breasts, stacking up piles of human heads to be seen by those who were soon to be so victimized, impaling people on stakes, tying rebellious kings with dog chains and forcing them to live in kennels. . . . The list of horrors goes on and on.

announcing the fall of his nation's long-time enemy. He was God's man of the moment, putting the overthrow of Nineveh into proper perspective.

Certain theological themes stand out in his brief book. First, for Nahum, God is sovereign Lord. His lordship over nature is evident. It is He who "rebukes the sea and dries it up" (1:4). Before Him "the blossoms of Lebanon fade" (1:4) and "the mountains quake" (1:5). The very earth itself "trembles at his presence" (1:5).

As sovereign Lord, He guides humanity's history. It is because of Him that the mightiest city of that day "will have no descendants" to bear its name (1:14). He is the one who will make Nineveh "a spectacle" (3:6). It is He who "will restore the splendor of Jacob" (2:2).

And yet Nahum does not express God's sovereignty only in terms of overwhelming power. The prophet also sees God's sovereignty in terms of righteousness. Rebellion against God means judgment, whereas reward comes to those who trust Him. Nahum thereby underscores that people are accountable for their choices.

Second, for Nahum, God is righteous judge. He relates to humanity on the basis of personal relationship to Himself. Judgment and salvation, in a sense, are two sides of the same coin. The one who relates to God in rebellion experiences judgment, whereas the one who relates in trust knows mercy.

Nineveh has plotted "against the LORD" (1:9). The people of the Assyrian capital are "vile" because they serve "carved images and cast idols" (1:14). They have no concern for morality. Their ethic is "wanton lust," which enslaves others by "prostitution" and "witchcraft" (3:4). Accordingly, God will consume the great city "like dry stubble" (1:10). His declaration to Nineveh is, "I am against you" (2:13; 3:5).

And yet at the same time, "he cares for those who trust in him" (1:7). In other words, whether one responds in trust and receives mercy or responds in rebellion and receives judgment, God's justice prevails.

A corollary to the theme that God is righteous judge is that militarism and tyranny have no legitimate place in this world. Such practices are self-destructive (see Matt. 26:52). God has no intention of granting violence free reign. Though innocent blood may be shed for a season, God will come in judgment.

Third, for Nahum, God is merciful Savior. He is tender and compassionate. He "is good, a refuge in times of trouble. He cares for those who trust in him" (1:7). Furthermore, He is patient with humanity, exceedingly "slow to anger" (1:3). To His people who suffer at the hands of wickedness, He promises ultimate deliverance: "Look, there on the mountains, the feet of one who brings good news, who proclaims peace! . . . No more will the wicked invade you; they will be completely destroyed" (1:15).

Chapter 2

The Picture of Nahum's God
(Nahum 1:1-15)

The first chapter of Nahum contains three major divisions: (A) The Title of the Book (1:1); (B) The Theological Foundation of the Prophet's Message (1:2-8); and (C) The Application of the Theological Truths (1:9-15).

Following the title in verse 1, the prophet introduces his message with a vivid description of God as the sovereign and righteous Lord. He is omnipotent, active in both history and nature, and just. In His awesome strength, those who trust Him find Him a safe refuge. But those who oppose Him find His power produces certain judgment.

This theological introduction to Nahum's sermon underscores the truth that a moral law undergirds history and the affairs of humanity. While God is remarkably patient, His character is such that His justice is inflexible. He is a merciful refuge; He is also the avenging Lord.

After placing his sermon in a legitimate theological context, Nahum begins his application in verses 9 through 15. Refuge is promised here to Judah, while judgment is inevitable for those who plot against God. The specific recipient of the judgment is not identified in this chapter (at least not within the text of the sermon; Nineveh is identified in the title). Perhaps the prophet keeps the identity hidden briefly for dramatic effect.[1] Viewing the chapter in context, the recipient of judgment is, of course, Nineveh.

---

[1]Nineveh is not mentioned by name in the sermon until Nahum 2:8. The translators of the NIV added the name in Nahum 1:8; 1:11; 1:14; and 2:1 for clarification.

A. The Title of the Book (1:1)

The prophets were proclaimers of God's Word. Their messages were first delivered to the people orally; later the messages were committed to writing. It is safe to conclude that if Nahum is responsible for the title of his book, it was added when the prophecy took on written character. It was not delivered by Nahum in his oral presentation.

Such titles are customary in Old Testament prophetic books. Nahum is unique, however, in that his title is the only one in the Old Testament that actually contains two specific titles in one. The first title reads, "An oracle concerning Nineveh," while the second says, "The book of the vision of Nahum the Elkoshite."

Some commentators see the existence of two titles as evidence of a later addition by another author. One of the titles, they argue, was the original; the other title was added later, perhaps when the so-called acrostic was appended to the book.

Perhaps a better approach is to recognize that the first title identifies the subject of the prophetic message. The second title, in turn, identifies the prophetic speaker. The two parts thus complement each other. Their incorporation within the written text by Nahum himself is certainly a reasonable possibility.

1. The Burden of Nineveh (1:1a)

The initial word in the Hebrew title of Nahum (*maśśā'*) has been the subject of some debate. Does the word simply identify a general prophetic literary form without regard to content? If so, it could be translated "an oracle," "an utterance," "a pronouncement," or "a prophecy." The LXX took this approach to the word.

Or does *maśśā'* denote a threatening, condemnatory prophetic announcement? If so, the proper translation would be "a burden," or "a sentence of doom." As a burden, heavy load, or weight of doom, the tone of such a message would be quite ominous.

The weight of evidence favors the translation "burden." First, this interpretation of *maśśā'* was used earlier in history than the translation "oracle."

Second, the etymological connections of *maśśā'* within the Hebrew language suggest the translation "burden." For example, it is derived from a Hebrew verbal root that means "to lift" and thus conveys the idea of lifting a load. Furthermore, another Hebrew noun spelled the same as the word in question comes from the same verb and is translated "heavy load" or "burden," referring to that which is carried by a camel or a mule.

Third, the word *maśśā'* occurs twenty-seven times in the Old Testament; it is always used in a context of judgment or threat, never before an announcement of salvation.[2]

Fourth, the word *maśśā'* never occurs in a phrase like "the *maśśā'* of Yahweh." If it simply meant "oracle" or "utterance," would it not be expected in such phrases? Were these prophetic messages not "the oracles of Yahweh"? Because *maśśā'* is never used this way, it emphasizes "burden" as the better translation.

These prophetic messages were not "the burdens of Yahweh." They were instead sentences of doom on those who deserved judgment. Thus Nahum's message concerning Nineveh is "a burden." It is the proclamation of God's ominous sentence of doom on "the city of blood."

While many see Nahum filled with hatred for Nineveh and gloating over its downfall, some commentators say the prophet spoke strictly out of his theological conviction that sin would be judged. Perhaps Nahum even felt that Nineveh's burden was, in a sense, his own. He may not have found great pleasure in pronouncing Nineveh's doom; he may have hurt just as God hurts over the plight of sinners. Yet as God's messenger in a specific historical moment, Nahum proclaimed faithfully the negative side of God's word. God's spokesmen must share His total message (see Acts 20:27); it was Nahum's lot to pronounce "a burden."

The sentence of doom Nahum pronounces concerned the most important city of the Assyrian empire. Nineveh, which was first occupied in prehistoric times, experienced its most significant period after Sennacherib (704–681 B.C.) made it his

---

[2] The twenty-seven uses are in prophetic books, with the exceptions of Proverbs 30:1 and 31:1. While some commentators have tried to interpret Zechariah 12:1 as an exception to the statement that *maśśā'* is always used in a threatening context, a close reading of that chapter reveals the judgment.

capital. During the reigns of his successors Esarhaddon (680–669 B.C.) and Asshurbanapal (668–627 B.C.), Nineveh was the world's greatest city. As indicated earlier, it was probably during this time that Nahum preached.

The Nineveh of this period was known for its untold wealth and cultural achievements. Its architecture was splendid, illustrated by world-famous palaces constructed for Sennacherib, Esarhaddon, and Asshurbanapal as well as by temples for the deities Ishtar and Nabu. Significant literary activity was encouraged by Asshurbanapal, who gathered a great library of clay tablets dealing with religion, astronomy, history, grammar, and mathematics.

But Nineveh was even better known for its negative qualities. Its brutality and cruelty had left a blood-path across the ancient world (see Nahum 3:19). Its wealth had been gathered by sacking and looting and by ruthlessly forcing taxes on captured peoples. Its idolatry was shameless, enticing many people with sensual fertility practices. Its kings were more than proud; they were arrogant beyond measure.

To this world-renowned city Nahum pronounced "the burden." Nineveh would be no more. The fall came in 612 B.C. to an army of Babylonians and Medes. In addition to the writings of Nahum and Zephaniah (see Zeph. 2:13–15), the Babylonian Chronicles, which are contemporary with the event, also tell the story. Though temporary settlements flourished briefly at the site, the great city never rose from its devastation. It became pasture land for grazing sheep, a heap of desolate ruin, which it still is today.

2. The Book of Nahum's Vision (1:1b)

Nahum's message about Nineveh, according to the complete title in verse 1, is a burden, a book, and a vision. The burden was Nineveh's; the book and the vision were Nahum's.

The only occurrence of the word "book" in the title of an Old Testament prophecy is here in Nahum 1:1. Some earlier commentators suggest this implies that the prophet wrote his vision without first speaking it to the people. Nothing, however, either within Nahum's text or external to it supports this position. Committing Nahum's prophecy to writing was merely another step in its eventual placement in the Old Testament canon. It was obviously a step taken for all of the canonical prophetic books, despite the omission of the precise word from their titles.

Nahum's message is also "a vision." This particular word is a technical term used for "a revelation" or "a prophecy" from God. It occurs also in the introductory verses of Isaiah and Obadiah. Its use here emphasizes the revelatory character of Nahum's message.

The Hebrew etymology of the word "vision" is significant. It comes from a verb that means "to see" or "to behold." The vision is thus "a seeing" or "a beholding." Another noun derived from the same verb is translated "a seer." It is one of the main words used in the Hebrew Old Testament to designate the prophets.

While the word in Nahum 1:1 could be interpreted as "a beholding," it does not necessarily mean that the prophet physically saw a vision. He could have seen a vision; however, the word could also mean that the prophet perceived God's revelation with the mind's eye. One's presuppositions about visionary experiences will influence interpretation at this point.

Though it is not certain *how* Nahum perceived the vision, it is abundantly clear that the vision was from God. The use of this technical word for prophecy verifies the message was not Nahum's creation. The prophet's ability to perceive Nineveh's future fall must not be credited to his astute political perception, even though he was certainly a man of keen awareness. Nahum's ability "to see" came from divine inspiration.

The final portion of the title identifies the prophet as "Nahum the Elkoshite." While the preceding chapter discussed both Nahum and his place of residence, suffice it to say here that the prophet from the rural community, with no significant family evident, with no long list of biographical accomplishments, is called forth by God at a strategic moment to preach a monumental message. How true it is that the heroes of the Bible are often those the world would never recognize.

B. The Theological Foundation of the Prophet's Message (1:2–8)

In delivering a sermon, the contemporary preacher moves from a theological truth to its application. Nahum did the same. He would make no exultant prediction of Nineveh's fall—at least not in the beginning of his sermon. Nahum wanted that announcement firmly rooted in concrete, theological realities. From these the proclamation of Nineveh's "burden" would be seen in proper perspective.

Nahum thus begins his sermon by reflecting on the nature and character of God. God is seen as sovereign, omnipotent, righteous, just, jealous, wrathful, and merciful. God did not create the world and leave it. He is continuously active in both nature and history. His vengeance is certain, but so is His mercy. These themes are intertwined in the prophet's theological introduction to his sermon.

1. The God of Vengeance (1:2–3b)

Old Testament writers used repetition to strengthen ideas. Clearly Nahum wanted to stress the theme of this brief but significant section: God's vengeance against His enemies is certain. Its execution may be delayed, but its certainty is never in doubt.

To emphasize this theme, Nahum repeatedly used the divine name "Yahweh." Translated as "the LORD" in the NIV, the name occurs ten times in the first chapter, with four occurrences in this brief section.[3] In other words, the prophet wanted his hearers to know unequivocally that Yahweh is a God of vengeance, wrath, and anger; He is a God of judgment.

Added to the repetition of the divine name is the emphasis on the dynamic activity of vengeance itself. This idea is reflected seven times in some way or another in these two brief verses: God is jealous; He is an avenging God or He takes vengeance (referred to three times); He is a God of wrath (referred to twice); and He is unwilling to leave the guilty unpunished.

---

[3] The word "Yahweh" occurs ten times in the first chapter, but the NIV recognizes only nine occurrences with its translation "the LORD." In Nahum 1:3c, it reads: "His way is in the whirlwind and the storm," whereas the Hebrew text literally reads: "Yahweh—in the whirlwind and the storm (is) his way."

This section in Nahum is closely related in form to several other Old Testament passages, including Exodus 34:6–7, Numbers 14:18, Psalm 103:8, and Psalm 145:8. Yet in these references the emphasis is on the positive dimension of God's love and mercy, whereas Nahum's emphasis is decidedly on the negative. For Nahum, Yahweh is a God of vengeance. According to the prophet, Yahweh acts in vengeance because He is a "jealous" God (1:2). The anthropomorphic character of this word needs to be underscored. God is not jealous as humans are jealous. For us, jealousy is a negative emotion, a feeling of envy toward another. God's jealousy is wrapped in His being the righteous creator of this world. Because it is God's world, He expects people to live in proper relationship with Himself and in accordance with His righteous character.

In that light, God demands to be the ultimate priority in human life. He wants no rival claiming our allegiance, commitment, and worship. The relationship with God must be central. Complete fidelity is expected; anything less will be neither accepted nor tolerated.

The Hebrew word for "jealous" (*qannô'*) may also have the connotation of "zealous"; it portrays divine zeal. God will not sit subdued when it comes to righteousness. He will act in no uncertain terms to maintain His righteous rulership in the world.

This jealous God will maintain the moral order of the world through the administration of His justice. That means to those who oppose Him, He will be the "avenging" God (1:2). The Hebrew word translated "avenging" in verse 2 is actually used three times in the original text. The NIV translates "vengeance" in two of those places. The word is a Hebrew form which can be translated either as a noun (avenger, vengeance) or as a verb (he avenges, he takes vengeance). A possible reading for the second verse is:

A jealous God and an avenger is Yahweh,
An avenger is Yahweh and an owner of wrath.

An avenger is Yahweh to His foes
And He Himself maintains (wrath) for His enemies.[4]

Just as jealousy is a negative human emotion, so also is vengeance. From our perspective, vengeance means revenge. We often picture the short-tempered person getting even with someone. The concept, when applied to God, however, has absolutely no character of malice, no vindictiveness. It is not a negative. Rather God, the righteous Lord, by His vengeance balances the scale of justice in the world. He vindicates His righteousness.

The Hebrew language had no form to express the superlative idea. When a writer wanted to note the superlative character of someone or something, he would often repeat the key word three times. Perhaps Nahum, by referring to God's vengeance three times in this verse, was trying to express the idea that God is the greatest avenger of all; He is the avenger of avengers. Is this not another way of saying that vengeance belongs to God?

In verse 3 Nahum says: "The LORD is slow to anger and great in power; the LORD will not leave the guilty unpunished." In the larger context of the book, some commentators feel that Nahum is here addressing a word to Judah rather than to Nineveh. It is suggested that some of the Judeans were having doubts about God in the midst of the Assyrian crisis, and Nahum here is trying to comfort them. In effect the prophet is telling the people that God is still patient with His people and will soon act on their behalf.

But that interpretation does not do justice to the theological intent of this section. Nahum's concern in verse 3ab is that God, merciful, yet jealous, is patient with all sinners for a time;

---

[4] The final line is difficult to translate. The verb can be translated "maintains," "keeps," or "guards," but precisely *what* Yahweh maintains is not said. The word is often used in agricultural situations with the connotation of guarding vineyards. Most commentators insert wrath in Nahum 1:2 (see the NIV), which is suggested by similar passages (see Ps. 103:9; Jer. 3:5) and is implied by the Nahumic context. (In line two, Yahweh is said to be the "owner" or "ruler" or "lord" or "master" or "possessor" of wrath.) However, in light of both the earlier discussion of God's jealousy and the variety of uses of the verb in question, perhaps the following translation of the line would be appropriate: "And He Himself maintains (the moral order) against His enemies." This reading also seems to be implied by the context.

however, judgment will indeed come if forgiveness is not sought. Wickedness, though perhaps left for a season, is still never condoned.

To apply Nahum's theological truth to the issue of Nineveh, one recognizes that God was most patient toward the wicked city. The judgment against Nineveh *could* have come decades before it did. But because of His patience and mercy, God waited, giving even corrupt Nineveh an unmerited extension of time. But no one should be deceived by God's patience. He will not let the guilty go free. They will be punished. The vengeance of God against His enemies is certain.

The emphasis on God's wrath and vengeance is not popular in our day. People want to reflect on the positive dimensions of the biblical story. But the negatives are a valid part of Scripture. Issues like God's vengeance remind us that His demands are real and must be taken seriously. Rebellion against God will be brought to judgment because God hates sin. He will never compromise in His relationship to it. He is the God of vengeance.

2. The Lord of Nature and History (1:3c–6)

In verse 3a Nahum declares that God is "great in power." This reading occurs nowhere else in the Bible. Some commentators, therefore, have changed it to the more common "great in mercy." This reading, of course, adds emphasis to the earlier "slow to anger," and both phrases underscore God's gracious patience.

But there is no valid reason to change the text. Nahum's meaning seems abundantly clear. God's slowness to anger, His delay in bringing vengeance on His enemies, is no sign of weakness or impotence. His patience reflects His mercy. By restraining His great power, He allows the wicked time for repentance. As the one "great in power," He remains in control. He will act in judgment on His own timetable.

To further exalt God's power, the prophet in verses 3c–5 appeals to several illustrations from nature. Echoes of historical events are heard in some of the examples.

For instance, God's awesome power is evident in the air (1:3cd). It is He who controls whirlwinds and storms, death-dealing acts of nature that can be used as instruments of judgment. Such phenomena are often Old Testament symbols for God's presence, power, and wrath.

Likewise the "clouds are the dust of his feet" (1:3d). Picture a warrior rushing into battle, pockets of dust rising from beneath his feet. For Nahum, the scene in the sky was like that, yet on a grander scale. The clouds themselves were the fine particles of dust raised by the feet of the great God as He hurried along in His wrath. As evidence of Nahum's literary skill, this graphic figure of speech is found nowhere else in the Bible.

In addition to the air, God's awesome power is evident in the world's waters (1:4ab). He controls the sea; He uses it for His own purpose. More than likely this is an allusion to God's victory at the sea in the Exodus event.

Rivers too are under His control. Here again Nahum probably makes an allusion to Israel's history. This time Nahum remembers the opening of the Jordan River when Israel entered the Promised Land under Joshua. The prophet generalizes his illustration; whereas it was the one river dried up in the earlier story, the God of Nahum has the ability to dry up all rivers.

Third, God's awesome power is evident on land (1:4c–5). Nahum mentions three places of great fertility to demonstrate God's omnipotence. Bashan, located east of the Jordan, was famous for its cattle, flocks, and trees. Carmel, the gardenlike mountain jutting out into the Mediterranean just below the modern city of Haifa, was known for its wooded heights and lush vegetation. Lebanon, north of Galilee, was famous for its snow-clad mountain summits and its stately cedars. These were the least likely areas in all of Palestine to show the effects of drought. But in the presence of the terrifying God, these places would quickly wither and fade.

Furthermore, the mountains and the hills, symbols of stability, would tremble and collapse before Him. Once again Nahum may be making an allusion, this time to the Sinai experience reflected in Exodus 19:18. While some commentators see here the backdrop of earthquake or volcanic activity,

Nahum poetically seems to envision tall mountains falling before the heavy step of the God of power.[5] The last half of verse 5 serves as a climax to the prophet's list of illustrations. Not only are the sea, the rivers, the places of great fertility, the mountains, and the hills affected by God's power but also the very earth itself "trembles at his presence" (1:5c).[6] His power overwhelms "the world and all who live in it" (1:5d), including all things animate and inanimate.

God's power is thus beyond human comprehension. He can use the forces of nature for His own purpose. He is the controlling factor in history. He is indeed the sovereign Lord of all. The terrible side of His nature is real.

Thus Nahum reaches the anguished but obvious conclusion: "Who can withstand his indignation? Who can endure his fierce anger?" (1:6ab). The answer to the rhetorical questions is, "No one." No opponent in all of the universe will ever succeed against this God. If the hard and immovable rocks of the earth are shattered by His presence, it is certain that His wrath will be an all-consuming fire (1:6cd).[7] No hope exists for those toward whom that wrath is directed.

3. The God of Refuge and Wrath (1:7–8)

Having illustrated God's unfathomable power, Nahum closes out the theological introduction of his sermon. The section is brief. Its message is clear.

God is not a capricious deity, who indiscriminately lashes out at humanity. He is the omnipotent, sovereign, righteous Lord. The moral order in this world is grounded in His nature. People either find refuge in God or they find judgment in Him.

---

[5]The NIV reads "the hills melt away" in verse 5, whereas the LXX says "the hills are shaken." The latter reading matches the imagery of the first part of the verse: "the mountains quake before him."

[6]The KJV reads: "the earth is burned at his presence." No evidence, either in ancient manuscripts or Hebrew etymology, substantiates this translation. The verb in the Hebrew text has a root meaning of "to lift up." The idea in Nahum 1:5 is that the earth "lifts itself up" or "heaves." From this comes the translation "trembles."

[7]Nahum's strong emphasis on God's wrath is seen in the Hebrew text of verse 6. Here the prophet uses four different words for the concept: indignation, fierce (this word, though used as an adjective in the NIV, is actually a noun form in Hebrew meaning "burning anger"), anger, and wrath.

One either trusts in God or finds oneself God's enemy. Because God is so strong, He is able to be either protector or judge, as is appropriate in every situation.

a. God's Relationship with His Friends (1:7). Nahum's text is brutally frank, even terrifying, through the first six verses. The lone exception is the brief statement of God's patience in verse 3, which appears in a section that emphasizes the certainty of judgment.

The first real positive word in Nahum comes in verse 7. Here the prophet points out three remarkable factors about God and His relationship with His people. The abruptness of the passage in the midst of a discussion of divine wrath seems to accentuate its joyful message.

First, God is "good" (1:7a). His goodness is reflected in many ways. He is good, for example, from a moral perspective in that He does not sin. He is good because of His fidelity; He is faithful to keep His promises. His goodness is often demonstrated in His mercy. As the psalmist wrote: "For you LORD are good and forgiving" (Ps. 86:5a).[8] It may not even be too far afield to suggest that God is happy, for the word "good" is frequently translated "happy" in the Old Testament.

Second, God is "a refuge in times of trouble" (1:7b). The image here is of the fortress or the stronghold for the soldier. When he is within its gates and behind its walls, he is safe from enemy attack. To leave its security is to face defeat. In the same sense, the only genuine security for people is in their relationship with God.

The "times of trouble" referred to here are not just the events of the last days, as some commentators suggest. Rather the phrase refers to all negative experiences of life.

It is sad that some commentators, while praising the nobility of Nahum's statement, see it as inaccurate. Some still believe that faith in God means that the believer will have no problems in life. Those who hold this view fail to understand this verse. God does not promise His people freedom from difficulties in this world. He instead promises His presence and sufficiency in the midst of difficulty. External situations may be

---

[8]This translation is by the commentary author.

devastating, but inner spiritual reality can still know God to be the valid refuge.

Third, God "cares for those who trust in him" (1:7c). The Hebrew text of this passage literally reads: "And He knows those who seek refuge in Him." The verb translated "knows" or "cares" is significant. Knowledge in a biblical sense is not so much head knowledge but heart knowledge; it refers to the intimacy of relationship. To know someone is to have a meaningful relationship with him or her. It is because God so intimately relates to His own that He provides care for them.

The last part of the verse—"those who seek refuge in Him"—is a vivid description of the biblical concept of faith and is rendered correctly in the NIV as "trust." Biblical faith has many dimensions. In addition to trust, faith calls for obedience. It means a total commitment of one's life to God. It means accepting that God receives us just as we are if we come to Him in confession and repentance. To those who seek refuge in Him, God is ever sufficient.

b. God's Relationship with His Enemies (1:8). The word "but" that begins this verse quickly reminds the reader that Nahum's main thrust is negative. Having announced the brief though marvelous promise to God's friends, the prophet returns now to the theme of judgment. Total destruction will come to those who are God's enemies.

But portions of verse 8 are difficult. The crux of the problem revolves around the translation of the last part of the second line, which is rendered by the NIV: "He will make an end of Nineveh." The Hebrew text reads at this point: "He will make a complete destruction of her place." Who is the "her" of this statement?

Many commentators opt for the reading given in the LXX: "He makes a full end of those who rise up against Him." This reading serves well as a parallel with the last line of the verse.

If the LXX version is accepted, the passage's purpose is to make a general statement that judgment is certain against all of God's enemies. In this case, the two figures "overwhelming flood" and "darkness" are simply symbols representing the confusion, hopelessness, and utter devastation of judgment.

If the Hebrew text is accepted, we are back to the identity of the "her." Commentators who have moved in this direction generally identify "her" as Nahum's first subtle reference to Nineveh in his sermon. In adopting this approach, verse 8 serves as a transition between the prophet's theological foundation and its application to his own day. While Nahum here still voices the general theological truth that God's judgment against His enemies is certain, at the same time he begins to merge theology with application. He begins to talk about Nineveh, albeit in a veiled way.

Accepting Nineveh's inclusion in verse 8 gives historical significance to the two figures. The overwhelming flood, for example, may refer to an event actually associated with the city's fall. Likewise the emphasis of God's foes being pursued "into darkness" may reflect Nineveh's total destruction.

In summary, Nahum's theological truth that God takes vengeance on His enemies is once again affirmed in verse 8. At the same time, the prophet, by his use of "her place," begins subtly to move his hearers to the application of his message— Nineveh's fall.

C. The Application of the Theological Truths (1:9–15)

In the last verses of the first chapter, Nahum moves specifically to applying his theology. Interestingly while the application of the positive message to Judah is clear, the application of the negative message to Nineveh is still veiled. Remember that the first mention of Nineveh by name in the text of the sermon does not come until Nahum 2:8.

Nahum alternates between God's judgment and His faithfulness in the last section of the chapter. To Nineveh there are threats reflecting the certainty of God's judgment against His enemies. To Judah there are promises reflecting God's faithfulness to His friends.

1. The Threat of Complete Destruction (1:9–12c)

Nahum initiates this new section of his sermon with another question, which he uses as an emphatic device. The prophet's previous questions came in verse 6 at the conclusion of a vivid description of God's awesome power. There Nahum had cried out: "Who can withstand his indignation? Who can endure his fierce anger?" Now addressing a still unnamed Nineveh,[9] the prophet asks: "What are you plotting against Yahweh?" (1:9a).[10]

He does not wait for an answer. None needs to be given. Anything "against Yahweh" is sin and subject to judgment.[11] And Nahum has already established that though God is "slow to anger," He "will not leave the guilty unpunished" (1:3ab).

Consequently the prophet assesses the success of Nineveh's plot and concludes that God will bring it "to an end" (1:9b). Here Nahum repeats the same tragic word he used a moment earlier in verse 8. There he declared that God would make "a complete destruction of her place." Once more the literary device of repetition for emphasis is at work. Be it Nineveh's place or its plots against God, the outcome will be "a complete destruction." God's judgment against the corrupt city is to be so thorough that it will not need to be repeated. It "will not come a second time" (1:9c).[12]

An extremely difficult verse to translate, verse 10 continues the theme of destruction. Here the prophet envisions Nineveh entangled among thorns and incapacitated by its drunken revelries. Both images describe a people incapable of standing before anyone, much less the awesome God of wrath. As dry stubble is easily consumed by raging fire, so Nineveh will be destroyed.

Nahum returns in verse 11 to the question he raised in verse 9. Here he reveals that Nineveh's plot "against the LORD" was evil and wickedness.[13] He attributes the sorry scheming to one

---

[9] Some commentators suggest that Nahum addresses Judah instead of Nineveh in verse 9 and that he is asking his own people why they doubt the Lord. However, the context seems to fit better the view that Nineveh is the addressee. The word used in verse 11 for Nineveh "plotting" evil is the same word translated "plot" in verse 9.

[10] The quote is the literal translation of the Hebrew. Notice the readings in the NIV text and footnote.

[11] Some theologians contend that the Old Testament nowhere deals with the sins of thought. The present passage is a good illustration to the contrary. Here we see the plotting, the imagination, the meditations of the Assyrians against God.

[12] Some commentators feel Nahum addresses Judah here, promising that Assyria will not come again with its armies to the Promised Land.

[13] The word translated "wickedness" is the Hebrew *belial*, a combination of the Hebrew words for "without" and "profit," hence the translation "without

who has "come forth" from Nineveh. Most scholars see this as a
reference to the Assyrian king Sennacherib and his invasion of
Judah in 701 B.C. Others think Nahum is offering a personification of all Assyrian rulers in the "one." No matter how one views
this issue, the passage is clear. Nineveh has plotted evil against
God. The outcome of such action is certain.

Verse 12 begins with the words: "This is what the LORD
says." Used only here in Nahum, this comment reiterates the
revelatory character of the message. It is not Nahum's word
against Nineveh; it is the word of the awesome God.

For the third time in this brief section, Nahum again
announces Nineveh's destruction. The city and its citizens "will
be cut down and pass away." The imagery used here is of
shearing sheep or cutting hair or mowing pastures. Nineveh will
be sheared until the city is no more. History reveals the
accuracy of Nahum's divinely inspired prediction.

2. The Promise of Deliverance (1:12d–13)

The last part of verse 12 represents a common problem
commentators have in chapter 1: the alternation of prophetic
messages to Nineveh and Judah. It is not always certain to
whom the prophet is speaking.

Some commentators suggest that verse 12d continues the
address to Nineveh begun in verse 9. If so, it would mean that
Nineveh would receive no further affliction from God, not
because of God's grace but because the city no longer exists. If
this approach is adopted, verse 12d can be seen as a parallel to
verse 9c.

The majority of translators, however, see verse 12d as a
promise to Judah. Notice that the NIV has actually inserted the
word "Judah" in the text. When Nahum wrote, Judah for years
had been a vassal state to the Assyrians, suffering greatly at the
latter's hand. This terrible time had indeed been God's affliction
on the nation ("I have afflicted you") because of rebellion

---

profit" or "worthlessness." The word came to be used for what is base and
villainous. Many commentators suggest that the word was also a proper name for
a demonic being (see 2 Cor. 6:15). If that is Nahum's meaning, it would seem
the prophet sees the conflict between God and His foes as not only historical but
also cosmic.

against Him. But now Nahum promises Judah that that affliction will be "no more."

Verse 12d must not be misunderstood. It does not mean that Judah would never again experience God's judgment. In fact an even greater judgment came at the hand of Babylon a few years after Nahum's message. The promise in verse 12, as is evident by the context, is that no more affliction would come *from Assyria*. And it did not!

Verse 13 contains a double promise. The figures of speech used in both promises are subject to debate among commentators. In the first promise, some see the instrument of judgment as the yoke worn by the beast of burden; others see it as the rod in the hand of the taskmaster. In the second promise, the illustration is either of shackles worn by prisoners or thongs attached to yokes. Although there is some uncertainty about the exact nature of the illustrations, there is none about the message: Judah will no longer suffer the indignities of Assyrian domination.

3. The Threat of No Future (1:14)

Once more Nineveh is addressed. Again Nahum identifies God as his authority for proclamation. And well he should. What mortal could see the long-term condition predicted in this verse? God had earlier declared the "complete destruction" of Nineveh, but now the matter is carried even further. The sovereign Lord of nations issues the divine decree ("command") that the corrupt city "will have no descendants" to perpetuate its name. Its fall will not be temporary; it will not be simply incapacitated for a season. Nineveh's fall will be permanent. This generation is Nineveh's last.

In verse 14 Nahum continues a catalog of Nineveh's sins that led to this tragic end. He had begun the list earlier when he described the plots of evil and wickedness against God (verses 9, 11), that is, the city's rebellion. The sin he now adds to the catalog is idolatry.

The Assyrians worshiped many deities, with Asshur, Ishtar, Nabu, Anu, Shamash, Adad, and Ninib among the most significant. Against the wrath of the true God these deities would prove their impotence. Their "carved images" (made from wood and stone) and their "cast idols" (made from metal) would be destroyed. Their temples would be desecrated, even as the Assyrians themselves had desecrated the worship centers of those they conquered.

The tragic verse closes with another statement of the doom and its cause. It is God who pronounces the doom: "I will prepare your grave." He Himself will bury Nineveh.

This figure emphasizes the annihilation that will soon occur. This judgment of the wrathful God comes because Nineveh is "vile." The Hebrew word used here means "to be light, slight, trifling." In other words, when Nineveh is evaluated on a moral basis, the city is "light," that is, morally deficient (see Dan. 5:27). Morality is grounded in the righteous God, whereas immorality results from rejecting Him. Nineveh's status as a moral lightweight is thus added to the catalog of sins that has led to God's sad word of extinction.

4. The Promise of Peace (1:15)

Nahum concludes the first chapter with a magnificent promise to Judah. For the first time in the text, one of the principal addressees is identified by name, and it seems no accident that such identification is now made. In many ways Nahum 1:15 is the book's key verse. Nahum's intention has been to announce Nineveh's end within the proper theological framework. Through this he desires both to comfort his people and to strengthen their relationship with God.

Now as if the destruction has already been accomplished, Nahum envisions a messenger on the nearby mountains. The messenger has run (notice the emphasis on "the feet") a considerable distance for days. Now he declares the "good news" that Assyria is no more. This indeed is a proclamation of peace (compare Isa. 52:7).

The Hebrew word for "peace" is one of the most remarkable words in that ancient biblical language. Its meaning is much more profound than simply the cessation of war. It refers to wholeness, completeness, total well-being.

It is not surprising to see Nahum turn immediately from the proclamation of peace to call Judah to grateful religious response. Certainly the nation's religious practices had been stymied for decades by Assyrian interference. Judah now had religious freedom, and Nahum wanted that freedom exercised responsibly. He therefore calls for a celebration of the festivals and advocates a fulfillment of vows. One can well imagine that many Judeans made vows to God during the time of Assyrian tyranny. Humanity often makes promises to God under stress and then forgets those promises when the stress is removed. Nahum reminds the people of their commitments.

The chapter closes with a reiteration of Nineveh's demise. The wicked city will indeed "be completely destroyed." Never again will Nineveh threaten Judah's existence.

Chapter 3

The Picture of Nineveh's Fall
(Nahum 2:1–3:19)

Chapters 2 and 3 of Nahum contain five major divisions: (A) The Siege and Capture of Nineveh (2:1–10); (B) The Sarcastic Question (2:11–13); (C) The Prophetic Woe of Judgment (3:1–7); (D) The Taunting Illustration of Destruction (3:8–13); and (E) The End of Nineveh (3:14–19).

The prophet's words throughout these chapters are filled with vivid imagery, electrifying scenes, and rapid movement. For those of us used to the modern movie screen, Nahum has unreeled a motion picture show of wicked Nineveh's last days.

A. The Siege and Capture of Nineveh (2:1–10)

Another mark of Nahum's effective literary style is the structure of this section. He begins (2:1) with a taunt to Nineveh that disaster is coming, but before he describes the disaster, he inserts a positive word to Judah (2:2). The pause seems to heighten the tension for Nineveh. Nahum then leaves the positive note to move rapidly through several verses, describing bluntly Nineveh's siege and capture (2:3–10). Some commentators believe that verse 2 is out of place and want to put it after Nahum 1:15. This type of textual rearrangement lessens the dramatic force of the prophet's writing.

1. The Taunt (2:1)

As Nahum turns once again to address Nineveh, he declares that "an attacker" is advancing against the great city. The Hebrew word found here is seldom used in the Old Testament.

It comes from a verb meaning "to disperse, to scatter"; hence, the noun form means "a disperser" or "a scatterer" or, as some commentators have suggested, "a dasher-in-pieces." Other commentators have made a slight change in the Hebrew word and consequently translate it as "a hammer," "a club or maul," or "a shatterer."

The prophet does not identify the attacker. From the historical perspective, the Babylonians and the Medes played the role. However, for Nahum, human armies were merely instruments in God's hand; He is the author of such events. In this light, it is interesting that the word for "attacker" in both its noun and verbal forms is almost always used for God in the Old Testament. In other words, the attacker may be the Babylonian-Median coalition on the historical level, but He is God on the larger theological level.

The interpretation of this verse as a taunt bothers some. They point out that the four commands ("guard the fortress," "watch the road," "brace yourselves," "marshal all your strength") would most likely be the words barked out by the Assyrian military leaders as the enemy advanced to the city. The argument is valid, but the words still serve as a taunt from Nahum's perspective. No matter how much watching and bracing the people of Nineveh do, this attacker is going to devastate them and their city.

2. The Positive Word to Judah (2:2)

The thrust of verse 2 is clear, though the specifics are not. In essence Nahum declares that, through Nineveh's fall, Judah will return to "the splendor" ("excellence," "majesty," or "pride," in the good sense) that it has not enjoyed since the "destroyers" ("plunderers") devastated the land, ruining the "vines." The vineyard imagery for Israel and Judah is common in the Old Testament.

The difficulty in the verse comes primarily because the meanings of the words "Jacob" and "Israel" are open to question. Each name can in turn symbolize the nation in its entirety, the northern kingdom, or the southern kingdom.

All kinds of interpretative possibilities are open, depending on the identification given each name. For example, the commentator who identifies "Jacob" as Judah and "Israel" as the northern kingdom is not going to reach the same conclusion as the one who identifies both names as representations of the nation in its twelve-tribe entirety.

As an example of the many interpretations, some commentators believe verse 2 is God's promise to restore politically both the southern kingdom and the northern kingdom (which of course did not happen). Others think God planned to restore politically both nations *through* the southern kingdom as the symbolic representation of the whole.

Perhaps the key to identifying the names comes from the theological perspective. Recall that Jacob the patriarch was a deceiver; when converted, he became Israel. The new name reflected Jacob's change of character when he became rightly related to God. What God may be saying here is that through the Assyrian crisis He has been working to bring Judah (living as Jacob the sinner) back to the status of Israel (one in right relationship with God).

3. *The Assault on Nineveh (2:3–10)*

The scene in the initial verse of this chapter was within Nineveh itself. There we heard the leadership barking out commands in anticipation of the assault. In Nahum 2:3 the scene shifts to Nineveh's attacker. Nahum's graphic description reveals how impressive this fighting force is.

The prophet first declares: "The shields of his soldiers are red" (2:3a). The identity of the "his" is not given but would be either the leadership of the attacking army (perhaps the appropriate general of the Babylonian-Median strike force) on the human level or God Himself on the theological level. Remember that this human attack force was God's instrument in judging Nineveh. The redness of the shields has been explained variously as a reference to: (1) the blood stains on the equipment of seasoned fighters; (2) the sunlight reflecting on the copper parts of the shields; or (3) the shields' leather or wood elements painted red.

Furthermore, Nahum describes "the warriors" of this great army as "clad in scarlet" (2:3b). The word translated "warriors" in the NIV is a combination of words in the Hebrew text, which literally translates "men of strength" or "men of valor" or "men of ability." The description fits a crack fighting force. Ezekiel later reports that the Babylonian army did indeed wear red whereas the Assyrians wore blue (see Ezek. 23:5–6, 14). Expanding the vivid scene from troops to weaponry, the prophet describes chariots and spears (2:3c–4). The enemy war chariots are seen racing "through the streets" and "squares" of Nineveh. The word translated "streets" means "the outside." This word and the context seem to imply that Nahum is describing the enemy chariots rushing through the suburban areas toward the wall of the great inner city. To Nineveh's army standing on the wall, the flash of sun on metal must have made the chariots seem to be "flaming torches" and bolts of "lightning." The added sight of enemy soldiers defiantly waving and shaking their spears ("the spears . . . are brandished") must have terrified Nineveh's defenders.

The scene appears to shift briefly at the outset of verse 5. Here Nahum reveals that an unidentified "he" summons his "picked troops." Some commentators feel the reference is to an Assyrian general *within* the city, whereas others believe this refers to one of the Babylonian-Median commanders *outside* the wall. The best troops from one side or the other are called to the critical city wall, the one for defensive purposes and the other for offensive.

As these troops move into place, "they stumble on their way" (2:5b). If one holds the view that the troops are Assyrian, then the reason for their stumbling is one of two factors: they either stumble because of their fear and uncertainty in the confusing, frightening situation, or they stumble because they are drunk. An ancient tradition suggests the Ninevites were intoxicated when their city was invaded.

If one identifies the troops of verse 5 as the Babylonians and Medes, then they too stumble for one of two reasons: they either stumble because of their eagerness to get to the fight, or they stumble because there are so many of them that they fall all over each other. Surely both their eagerness and their number would have terrified the people of Nineveh.

When the soldiers reach the city wall, "the protective shield is put in place" (2:5d). If the first part of verse 5 is indeed a reference to Ninevite defenders, then the last part of the verse focuses on the action of the Babylonian-Median coalition, most commentators believe. In other words, it is the enemy *outside* the walls who situates the protective shields.

The word used here is literally translated "a covering" or "a protection." It evidently describes a weapon the ancients developed for breaching walls. Archaeologists have discovered evidence of this ancient weapon that consisted of a wooden tower on four to six wheels. The tower contained several stories on which soldiers would stand. A battering ram was often attached to the structure. The entire machine was covered to protect the soldiers from rocks and other objects thrown at them from the walls above.

In verse 6 Nahum's emphasis changes once again. He has been describing the army of Nineveh's attacker, its eagerness to do battle, its advance to the city walls, and its deployment of weaponry. Now the prophet begins to describe the actual invasion of the proud Assyrian capital.

The event that allowed the invasion to occur is reported in the phrase "the river gates are thrown open" (2:6a). The meaning of this passage has been clarified by archaeology.

It is now known that Sennacherib developed in Nineveh a massive flood-control program that included building dams and flood gates, creating reservoirs, and even changing river courses. He was especially determined to control the two rivers that flowed through Nineveh itself, the Tebiltu and the Khosr.

On the basis of Nahum 2:6, the Babylonian-Median forces evidently opened the various flood gates and thus submerged large sections of the city, making it impossible to defend. In addition, the onrushing water did major structural damage to buildings in the city ("and the palace collapses," 2:6b).

Two significant factors stand out. First, an old Assyrian legend asserted that Nineveh would never fall unless the river became its enemy. Second, Nineveh's overthrow came at the season of the greatest rainfall, when the rivers were at their highest. The high waters which opened Nineveh to the invaders give us an example of God using nature for His own purpose.

The first half of verse 7 is the most difficult passage in this section. The NIV reads: "It is decreed that the city be exiled and carried away." The Hebrew text, on the other hand, literally translates: "And Huzzab is uncovered, carried away." The meaning of the Hebrew *Huzzab* is indiscernible. Some scholars interpret the word to be the name of the Assyrian queen or the name of some priestess of Ishtar. Others interpret it as a symbol for Nineveh or Assyria. Numerous other interpretations have been offered, including that of the NIV translators and others that the word should be rendered as a verbal unit: "it is decreed." In light of the limited evidence, the matter must be left unsolved for now.

If *Huzzab* is the Assyrian queen, the "slave girls" of verse 7b are the women of her court. Seeing their mistress stripped and carried away by the invaders they "moan like doves" (the sound of the dove's cooing reminds one of mourning) and "beat upon their breasts" (a symbol in the ancient world to express grief). If *Huzzab* is Nineveh, the "slave girls" symbolize the city's women who see their men dying in battle all around them and bemoan their fate.

The emphasis on the queen or the city being carried away in verse 7 is continued in verse 8. Here Nahum compares Nineveh to "a pool" and envisions "its water . . . draining away" (2:8ab). The prophet's figure of speech may reflect that Nineveh was like a pool fed by many tributaries. Many people from all over the ancient world had poured into the city because of its enormous wealth and economic opportunities. But now in the day of defeat, the people ("its water") are fleeing as fast as they can. As they run, someone, perhaps a military officer, demands that they "Stop!" "But no one turns back" (2:8cd).

By the conclusion of verse 8, the scene in Nineveh is chaotic: water rushes through the streets, frightened women moan in agony, invading soldiers kill indiscriminately, people run and trip all over each other trying to escape. In the confusion and panic, the looting and the pillaging begin (2:9). From house to store, from palace to temple hurry the looters, taking the "silver" and the "gold" and the "endless . . . treasures."

Nineveh was no doubt the world's richest city of that day. Its wealth was acquired through its evil. Now its wealth was being taken. This verse surely reflects yet another sin of Nineveh to add to Nahum's catalog: the sin of materialism.

The final verse of this section (2:10) is a literary master-piece. It begins with what is a powerful paronomasia (a play on the sound of words) in the Hebrew. Unfortunately the effect of this play on words is lost in our English translation. The NIV reads: "She is pillaged, plundered, stripped." In the Hebrew the three words sound alike, with each word a little longer than the one that precedes it; they all have similar meanings. Their usage as a unit emphasizes how totally pillaged and plundered Nineveh is when the assault is over. The scene fades with Nahum using four striking statements (2:10bc) to describe the devastated emotions of the defeated Ninevites as they stagger through the wreckage of their once-powerful city.

B. The Sarcastic Question (2:11–13)

As we have seen, questions are one of Nahum's favorite literary devices. This section opens with a taunting, mocking question: "Where now is the lions' den . . . ?" (2:11). Where now is the city of Nineveh? Where now is the place of undisturbed peace (see the phrase "with nothing to fear" in verse 11d)? The hearer knows the answer well. Nineveh is nowhere! The great city has been destroyed.

As to be expected from a product of divine inspiration, Nahum's predictive words have been exceedingly precise. Nineveh's devastation was so thorough that for centuries people would pass its ruins not even knowing what it was they passed. The mounds that stood on the site were not unmistakably identified until the middle of the last century. Even now with all of the archaeological investigation done in the area, the exact boundaries of Nineveh have not been decided.

Nahum's use of lion imagery for Nineveh in this brief section is quite appropriate. Not only was the lion a common symbol for Israel's foes in the Old Testament, but also the lion as a ravenous beast was an apt symbol for brutal Nineveh. Furthermore, the lion was frequently used in Assyrian art. Archaeologists have discovered numerous lion sculptures, some winged, some unwinged. These figures were often associated with Assyrian deities, leading to the suspicion that Nahum's implications in this section were once again on two levels. On one hand, the prophet envisions God's judgment in history on a human enemy; on the other hand, God defeats Nineveh's gods and thus the cosmic forces of evil.

The lion imagery is continued in verse 12. Here Nahum describes the viciousness of the lion's attack on its prey. The den is filled for the benefit of the lioness and cubs. Another sin for Nahum's catalog is vividly illustrated here. Nineveh was famous for its inhumanity to others. Just as the lion ravaged and killed and carried home its prey, so also did the Assyrian troops. They literally filled Nineveh with war booty on which all its citizenry then thrived.[1] But now the lions' den is gone!

The reason for the city's disappearance is certain. Nineveh ran afoul of God. Her sinfulness led to history's most tragic pronouncement: " 'I am against you,' declares the LORD Almighty" (2:13a). The theological undergirdings of the sermon resurface here.

Four evidences of the judgment conclude the section. First, Nineveh's chariots, representing the best of its weaponry, will be burned (2:13b). Second, the city's young will be destroyed (2:13c); an echo of the earlier threat in Nahum 1:14 is heard here. Third, Nineveh will have "no prey on the earth" (2:13d); never again will Assyrian soldiers plunder neighboring nations. Fourth, the voices of Nineveh's messengers will be stilled (2:13e); Nahum is thinking perhaps of men like Rabshakeh (2 Kings 18:19–35), who made Assyrian demands for submission and tribute known among captured peoples. Because of the awesome God's wrath, Nineveh's end, vividly described in the earlier verses of chapter 2, has come.

C. The Prophetic Woe of Judgment (3:1–7)

Chapter 3 begins with the significant word "woe" (Hebrew *hôy*), which is used to express pain and dissatisfaction. Other possible translations include: "O!" or "Ho!" or "Ah!" or "Alas!" or "Ha!" The Old Testament contains fifty-one occurrences of this word (fifty in the prophets), forty of them introducing warnings of judgment and physical chastisement. A survey of

---

[1] Notice four different kinds of lions mentioned in Nahum's illustration: lion, lioness, young lion, and cub. Represented here is the entire pride of lions, hence, the entire city of Nineveh.

these passages underscores the finality of judgment when the prophetic "woe" is pronounced.

Interestingly enough, another Hebrew word for "woe" (*'ôy*) is considered a much harder term. The word used by Nahum has a touch of pity and sympathy. Perhaps Nahum used *hôy* instead of *'ôy* to express his hurt (and God's hurt) regarding Nineveh's tragic end.

That end was the inevitable result of sin. Nineveh's wrongs against God and other people form a major part of the prophetic message after the mention of plots against Yahweh in Nahum 1:9. Here the prophet continues the catalog of the city's rebellion, mentioning the sins of militarism and deceit (3:1).[2]

Three graphic phrases illustrate Nineveh's militarism. First, Nineveh was "the city of blood." The word "blood" is plural in Hebrew; this gives the idea of "blood on blood" and thus magnifies the widespread violence and carnage that came from Nineveh's military actions.

Second, Nineveh was "full of plunder." To interpret "plunder" simply as the spoils of war is to miss Nahum's point. The Hebrew word the prophet uses speaks more to the savagery and inhumanity employed to obtain plunder. The term connotes "snatching away" or "tearing in pieces." It reminds one of a lion's action and may mean that Nahum is still reflecting on his earlier illustration in chapter 2:11–13.

Third, Nineveh was "never without victims!" The emphasis is not so much on the number of victims available for the militaristic city to overthrow but rather that Nineveh's continuous practice was to make victims of others. History bears out that Assyria, particularly in its later history, was usually involved in war.

Having again established the rightness of Nineveh's destruction, Nahum describes for a second time the final assault on the city (3:2–3). In rapid, staccato fashion, the drama unfolds before the reader. One first *hears* "the crack of whips, the clatter of wheels," the "galloping horses and jolting chariots!" The invading army suddenly appears and one *sees* "charging cavalry, flashing swords and glittering spears!" And the results in

---

[2]Nineveh's deceit is reflected in the phrase "full of lies," which the Hebrew literally presents as "all of it [the city] is a lie."

Nineveh are horrifying—"many casualties, piles of dead, bodies without number, people stumbling over the corpses. . . ."

Retributive justice runs throughout Nahum's sermon. He gives numerous examples of the Ninevites receiving in judgment the same terrors they had caused others to suffer. Assyrian records show they flooded many cities; so Nineveh is now flooded (2:6). They carried people from their homelands; so Nineveh is carried away (2:7). They plundered their enemies' treasures; so Nineveh's treasures are plundered (2:9). They left their victims shattered emotionally; now their "hearts melt" (2:10). They left "bodies without number" in a host of devastated cities; now Nineveh has its "piles of dead" (3:3). Certainly our sins come back to haunt us!

In the first three verses of the chapter, Nahum skillfully contrasts Nineveh's sins with the tragic price it paid for them. Nahum balances an emphasis on sin (3:1) with a section on judgment (3:2–3). In verse 4, Nahum returns to the issue of sin. Here he describes Nineveh as "a harlot" who has "enslaved nations by her prostitution and peoples by her witchcraft."

Commentators differ on the exact nature of the sin referred to here. Some point out that harlotry is often used in the Old Testament to describe Israel's idolatry, but most commentators feel that is not the issue here. Some commentators believe verse 4 refers to Assyrian occult practices, though this is questionable. The majority see the verse as a reference to the various vile practices Nineveh used to subjugate its neighbors.

Regardless of the sin's specific nature, Nahum returns to the issue of judgment in verses 5 to 7. For the second time the prophet shares God's negative word to Nineveh: "I am against you" (3:5a). This repetition of Nahum 2:13 magnifies its certainty.

Three aspects of God's negative declaration are then announced. First, Nineveh is to be exposed before the world (3:5). The passage may reflect the ancient world's treatment of prostitutes or the Assyrian practice of stripping and degrading prisoners of war. The verse's message is that Nineveh will be seen for what it really is.

Second, Nineveh is both to be treated with disrespect and to be rejected (3:6). This is the only mention in the Old Testament of throwing filth at prostitutes; the passage probably reflects an unwritten practice either in Israel or the ancient Near Eastern world. To throw filth on a person expressed utter contempt. Thus the city is made a "spectacle."

Third, Nineveh is to be deserted and isolated (3:7). In the day of ruin, the city will have no friends. Everyone will flee from it because it is an object of disgust, and everyone will fear being caught up in its ruin. No one will mourn for the city. There will be no one to comfort it.

Perhaps there is a trace of sorrow in Nahum's closing questions. Even wicked Nineveh should have someone to lament its end. Even Nineveh needs a comforter in the day of devastation. But the city's cruelty alienated everyone from it. Its tragic hour comes in isolation.[3]

D. The Taunting Illustration of Destruction (3:8–13)

If those who heard the sermon doubted the prediction of Nineveh's fate, Nahum was quick to remind them of the recent overthrow of another awe-inspiring city, the Egyptian royal city of Thebes (3:8–10). In 663 B.C. Thebes was soundly defeated by the Assyrians under Asshurbanapal.

Thebes was located 450 miles south of modern Cairo. Situated on both banks of the Nile (3:8ab), this impressive city had been important to Egyptian culture for more than 1,400 years. In fact, in Egyptian records, Thebes was designated as "the city." Archaeological investigation reveals Thebes was twenty-seven miles in circumference. The Pharaohs of the Eighteenth, Nineteenth, and Twentieth Dynasties made Thebes their capital and beautified it with booty from their wars.

With its strategic location on the Nile, Thebes had thought itself invincible. "The river was her defense, the waters her wall" (3:8de). The Nile at Thebes is about half a mile wide and is divided into various branches. Manmade channels, canals, and moats regulated the water. In a very real sense Thebes had

---

[3] I contend that Nahum felt strong compassion for people, even the wicked Ninevites. He was not the bloodthirsty, revenge-seeking, cold-hearted nationalist so many accuse him of being. Hints of this compassion can be found in the discussions of the words "burden" in Nahum 1:1 and "woe" in Nahum 3:1, as well as in the present passage. See also note 5 below.

"water around her" (3:8c), though this should not be interpreted literally to mean the city was on an island.

In addition to the advantageous location, Thebes was supported by powerful allies (3:9). To the south was Cush, which today includes much of what is Sudan and Ethiopia. The Ethiopians were in fact the rulers of Egypt when Thebes fell in 663 B.C. To the north of Thebes was Egypt proper and to the west was Libya. The location of the other ally—Put (perhaps the Punt of Egyptian inscriptions)—is uncertain. Most think the word refers to what is today the Somali Republic. The thrust of Nahum's description seems clear: Thebes had powerful allies on every side.

And yet the great Egyptian city was crushed by Nineveh (3:10)! Nahum's description at this point vividly brings to mind the catalog of sins committed by Nineveh. Its militarism, inhumanity, and materialism are illustrated in its treatment of fallen Thebes. The citizens of Thebes were captured and taken into exile. Because the infants and small children were an inconvenience to the Assyrian soldiers on the long journey, the soldiers murdered the children by smashing their heads against stones or walls. This barbaric practice was done "at the head of every street." In other words, the soldiers murdered children in public view to demonstrate Assyrian domination.

Another indignity inflicted on captured Thebes involved the nobility. These upper-class persons were valued for their education and experience, and to own such a person would give economic advantage. Thus the Assyrian soldiers gambled ("lots were cast") for these select people. Those who won them led them away "in chains."

In light of the Theban disaster, Nahum, speaking to Nineveh at the outset of this section, raises yet another of his rhetorical questions. In taunting fashion he asks: "Are you better than Thebes . . . ?" Are you better situated? Do you have stronger allies? The unspoken answer was an unqualified "No!" As Thebes fell, so would Nineveh.

In verses 11, 12, and 13 Nahum pinpoints four reasons why Nineveh would fall. The first reason is that Nineveh "will become drunk"(3:11a). Opinions vary as to the exact meaning of the prophet's statement. Some commentators believe he means

that Nineveh is intoxicated by its own power, its self-centeredness, its pride, its feeling of superiority that led to the belief it
could not be beaten. Such pride obviously leads to failure.

Other commentators maintain Nahum is using the figure of
speech to emphasize the loss of one's senses under the kind of
catastrophe that now befalls Nineveh. Still others believe the
reference is to the tradition that the Ninevites were drunk on the
day of their destruction. Perhaps the best interpretation is that
Nineveh will become drunk on the cup of God's wrath (see Isa.
51:17). It is God who staggers the city with His judgment.
Because of His action, Nineveh "will go into hiding" (3:11b), or
better, Nineveh "will be hidden"—hidden for centuries under
the ruins of destruction![4]

Second, Nineveh will fall because its "fortresses are like fig
trees" (3:12a). Soldiers used the fortresses to guard the ap-
proaches to the city. Nahum's figure of speech may have a
double meaning. It may refer to the enemy's eagerness to
devour Nineveh's fortresses, even as the person deprived of
fruit during the cold winter is eager to eat the first ripe fruit of
spring (3:12b). Or the figure may refer to the ease by which the
fortresses are destroyed. Their destruction will be no more
difficult than shaking ripe fruit from a tree (3:12cd).

Third, Nineveh will fall because her troops have become
"women" (3:13ab). In other words, the once-feared army will
now itself be fearful, hesitant to fight, and thus subject to defeat.
The old fighting spirit that characterized campaigns like the one
against Thebes is lost in the face of certain defeat.

Fourth, Nineveh will fall because "the gates" of the land
"are wide open" to the enemy (3:13cd). This refers to both the
fortifications guarding the mountain passes into the country and
the other defensive sites. These fortifications now have been
overrun and left burning (3:13e). The enemy hurries to the great
city itself!

As Lord of history, God clearly had punished Thebes for its
rebellion against Him. Assyria had been the instrument in His
hand for that punitive action, but Nineveh failed to learn the
lesson from Thebes. Now like Thebes, the great Assyrian city

---

[4]The last line of Nahum 3:11 (you will "seek refuge from the enemy") implies
that Nineveh has no refuge. That idea certainly fits the book's larger context.

lived in rebellion against God. And like Thebes, Nineveh's end now was in sight.

E. The End of Nineveh (3:14–19)

At the conclusion of the last section, Nahum envisions Nineveh's fortresses overrun and in flames. The enemy army quickly approached the great city. In taunting fashion, the prophet now calls for the Ninevites to prepare for the siege (3:14). The outer defenses have fallen; the people must now hold out in the inner city.

Nahum's first piece of ironic advice to Nineveh is: "Draw water for the siege" (3:14a). A few commentators contend that the prophet is instructing the Ninevites to fill the moats surrounding the city as a defensive measure. The verb "to draw," however, is used generally for securing drinking water from a well. A long siege was expected, and a large supply of water was an absolute necessity.

Nahum next commands: "Strengthen your defenses" (3:14b). This does not refer to the fortifications outside the city, which had already been destroyed by the invaders. It is rather a call to strengthen the wall, the towers, and other fortifications within the inner city itself. Obviously the enemy would use battering rams to try to break through the wall, which would be in need of constant repair throughout the siege. Such repairs could not be made without a steady flow of new bricks; thus Nahum speaks to this issue in the three closing lines of verse 14: "Work the clay, tread the mortar, repair the brickwork!"

But no matter how disciplined the Ninevites' effort, it will not be enough. As they attempt to defend the inner city, they will be overrun by the advancing enemy. "There the fire will devour you; the sword will cut you down" (3:15ab). Nineveh's buildings will be destroyed by fire while the people die by the sword. Ancient historians report that the king at the time of Nineveh's fall burned himself and his family alive in the palace to avoid capture by the enemy. Archaeological investigation reveals extensive fire damage in the city's ruins; a prime example was the scorched and blistered tablets found in Asshurbanapal's library.

In addition to fire and sword, Nahum discusses Nineveh's

total destruction with the image of the locust (3:15c). Locust invasions were highly feared in the ancient world because fields and vineyards would be completely stripped by these insects. So, warns Nahum, will Nineveh be totally consumed.

The prophet then makes a sudden but interesting turn. Having used the locust as a symbol *against* Nineveh, he now identifies Nineveh itself *with* the locust. The locust was known for its vast numbers, its devastating actions, and its sudden disappearance. According to Nahum, all these characteristics fit Nineveh well.

First, Nineveh prided itself on and found great hope in its sheer numbers. Nahum notes the multiplicity of the people (3:15de), the merchants (3:16), and the leadership (3:17). Second, vast numbers of merchants flocked to the city during the good times, but now in the face of disaster they "strip the land" and "fly away" (3:16). Third, just as locusts suddenly disappear, so also will Nineveh. Like the merchants, various leaders, who had settled in like the locust "on a cold day," hurried away and disappeared in the heat of the conflagration (3:17).

In the sermon's final paragraph, Nahum taunts the Assyrian king (3:18–19). He notes first that the empire's leaders ("your shepherds," or rulers, and "your nobles") are now dead (they "slumber" and "lie down to rest"). Without leadership the people who escaped the sword are "scattered on the mountains" to the city's north. No one remains around whom they can rally. The wound suffered by Nineveh is fatal. Nothing can be done now to save the wicked city.[5]

Then with yet another rhetorical question, Nahum brings the sermon to an end (3:19c). To Nineveh he says: "Everyone who hears the news about you claps his hands at your fall, for who has not felt your endless cruelty?" When the world learns of Nineveh's destruction, unusual rejoicing takes place, for all have suffered—and suffered continuously—at the wicked city's hand. The world receives news of Nineveh's end with ecstatic joy.

---

[5]One senses the prophet's feeling of powerlessness in the face of Nineveh's great need in Nahum 3:18–19ab. Though the section is framed for literary reasons in the form of irony and taunt, the passage seems to reflect sadness in the prophet's heart. No person should ever preach eternal judgment with joy.

Nahum's sermon has announced that the tyrant is no more. Despite the power and resources of mighty Nineveh, the day of destruction has come. The sovereign God is still in control; He reigns as the Lord of history. In this reality is our hope!

For Further Study on Nahum

1. In a Bible dictionary or encyclopedia, read articles about: Nineveh, Assyria, Sennacherib, Esarhaddon, and Asshurbanapal.

2. What do you feel Nahum's theological emphasis on God's wrath says about the responsibility one has in personal evangelism?

3. In a Bible dictionary or encyclopedia, read articles about: Israel, Judah, and Jacob, recalling especially our discussion of Nahum 2:2.

4. What danger do you see for us today regarding the various sins Nahum listed as Nineveh's?

5. Some commentators argue that the Book of Nahum has no theological value. Do you agree with this conclusion? Why or why not?

6. If God rules all nations, what does that mean for nations today?

7. How do you respond to the author's conclusion that Nahum had compassion for Nineveh?

Chapter 4

An Introduction to Habakkuk and His Prophecy

The catastrophic events of the last decades of the seventh century B.C. and the first decades of the sixth century B.C. left many people reeling and disillusioned. It was an agitated time, characterized by rapid political change, international turmoil, bloody military encounters, and a growing rebellion against the demands of the covenant by the great majority in Judah. Prophetic activity was feverish, not only with the ministries of people like Jeremiah, Nahum, Zephaniah, Huldah, and Ezekiel, but also with false prophets in abundance.

It is not surprising that in a time of such uncertainty a prophet with an unorthodox approach should appear on the scene. Habakkuk adopted the role of the philosopher of religion, seeking to understand the troubling times in light of his theological heritage. His approach was unique among canonical Old Testament prophets. Whereas his colleagues served primarily as messengers from God to the people, Habakkuk took the concerns that troubled him and his fellow citizens to God.

The key issue on this man's sensitive heart was theodicy: how can evil exist if God is good, just, and sovereign? Life's injustices troubled Habakkuk greatly. The very presence of evil was a problem for his faith. How could wickedness be allowed to continue unchecked? How could the wicked be allowed to devastate "those more righteous than themselves" (1:13)? In agonizing struggle, Habakkuk honestly and openly challenged God to answer.

And God responded to him. Though the divine response

did not settle the intellectual problem for Habakkuk, it satisfied him and brought him assurance for positive living. He saw that God is in control, that evil is ultimately doomed, and that the righteous will prevail. Though his world remained deeply troubled, Habakkuk was able to trade his doubts and speculations for confident trust and joyful worship. His faith had been sorely tried, but his story ends with faith intact and triumphant. He had learned the way of victorious living. In a world still dominated by evil, we do well to learn from Habakkuk's experience.

A. Habakkuk the Man

The only reliable information we have on Habakkuk is contained in the book that bears his name—and it is limited at best. Though his writings are quoted several times in the New Testament, he is not mentioned there by name (Acts 13:41; Rom. 1:17; Gal. 3:11; Heb. 10:37–38). The canonical material is silent on Habakkuk's genealogy, birthplace, and death, though numerous legends have grown up in an effort to fill in the gaps. The origins of the various legends are obscure; they certainly cannot be trusted as historically reliable. We are left with three short chapters and a few clues from which to uncover the prophet's life.

1. Habakkuk's Name

The prophet's name occurs in Habakkuk 1:1 and 3:1; it appears nowhere else in the Bible. It is given as Ambakouk in the LXX and Habacuc in the Vulgate. The Hebrew form is unusual; it is certainly not a normal Hebrew word.

Uncertainty persists about the name's origin or etymology. Some grammarians see it as Hebraic, coming from a verbal root that means "to embrace, to caress, to clasp." If so, the noun form could mean "embrace," "ardent embrace" (due to its intensive form), "the one who is embraced" (or "darling"), "the one who embraces," or even, according to Jerome, "the wrestler."

Others see Habakkuk's name as foreign in origin. It has been associated with the Assyrian word *hambakuku*, which was the name of a flower, garden plant, vegetable, or fruit tree. A minority opinion relates it to the Arabic word *hibhkatun*, which means "dwarf."

If the Hebrew origin is correct, several possibilities exist as to the significance of the name for Habakkuk's life and ministry: (1) It may refer either to his embracing or loving God or embracing and comforting his fellow Judeans. (2) It may reflect his parents' hope that he would embrace God. (3) It may describe his spiritual struggle or wrestling with God. (4) It may indicate that he was embraced by God.

If the name is of Assyrian origin, the following questions are appropriate: (1) Does Habakkuk's name reveal the Mesopotamian influence in Judah at that time? (2) Was he perhaps a foreigner who was converted? (3) Was he the child of a Judean-Assyrian mixed marriage? Habakkuk's name unfortunately raises more questions than it answers.

2. Habakkuk's Home

The biblical material provides no information about Habakkuk's birthplace. A legend from a fourth-century source entitled the *Lives of the Prophets* identifies Bethzochar or Bethzachar as the prophet's home. This was probably Beth-Zachariah, located ten miles southwest of Jerusalem (see 1 Maccabees 6:32).

A few writers point to the possible Assyrian origin of Habakkuk's name to contend that he was either from Assyria or a Judean in captivity in Mesopotamia. Some would carry this argument so far as to give Habakkuk an Assyrian education and to place his ministry in Assyria, perhaps at Nineveh.

However, most interpreters believe the prophet was a Judean whose ministry was concentrated in Jerusalem. Certainly the book's context would lead to this conclusion. The musical dimensions of chapter 3 alone point to temple worship and ministry in the Holy City.

3. Habakkuk's Date

Old Testament prophetic books occasionally have chronological information in their titles. Unfortunately such is not the case with Habakkuk.

Commentators generally assign the book to the late seventh century B.C. due to two clues. First, Habakkuk stands between Nahum and Zephaniah, both thought to be from the last decades of the seventh century B.C. Some evidence exists that the twelve minor prophets were arranged chronologically. Second, the reference to the Babylonians in Habakkuk 1:6 is usually identified with the Neo-Babylonian empire that came to power after 625 B.C.

A few writers place the book elsewhere in time. Some date it as early as the last quarter of the eighth century, in either the reigns of Ahaz or Hezekiah and contemporary with Isaiah. Others see the reference to violence in Habakkuk 1:2–4 as a reflection of Manasseh's reign (687–642 B.C.). On the other extreme are those who place the book in exilic times or even later. Some place it in the age of Alexander the Great around 330 B.C. (they change "Babylonians" in 1:6 to "Kittim," which refers to the Greeks). Some suggest that Habakkuk is from the period of Antiochus Epiphanes (about 170 B.C.). This last position totally ignores the reference to the book of the twelve prophets (which certainly included Habakkuk) made by Ben Sira in 180 B.C. (see Ecclesiasticus 49:10); this position thus must be rejected.

No unanimity exists among scholars who place Habakkuk in the late seventh century. Some put him in the last years of Josiah's reign (640–609 B.C.), while others date him either in the pre-Carchemish (609–605 B.C.) or post-Carchemish (605–598 B.C.) years of Jehoiakim.

I think it is better to interpret the violence of 1:2–4 as characteristic of Jehoiakim's reign rather than Josiah's. But whether Habakkuk wrote before the famous battle of Carchemish or afterward is difficult, if not impossible, to decide. In 1:5–6 the prophet predicts that God will raise up the Babylonians as agents to punish Judah; but then in 1:7–11 he seems to know by eyewitness observation their ferocious methods of warfare.

Does this mean the battle of Carchemish had been fought? Perhaps Habakkuk wrote after Carchemish and in 1:5–6 is looking back rather than predicting. Or perhaps these seemingly contradictory passages reflect different occasions of writing, whereas the book obviously represents the final compilation of materials. At any rate, I believe it is best to date the book as it stands in the post-Carchemish days of Jehoiakim, perhaps about 600 B.C.

4. Habakkuk's Occupation

Evidence links Habakkuk to Judah's official religious establishment. While the canonical prophets at times stood outside the formal worship structure (see Amos 7:14), Habakkuk may have been a professional worship leader. He may have participated, perhaps on a regular basis, in temple rituals, serving either as prophet, priest, or temple singer. Some of the evidence offered for this conclusion is questionable, but several factors make the case at least plausible.

First, Habakkuk is called a prophet (*nābhî'*) in both the superscription of the book (1:1) and in the title to the concluding psalm (3:1). Only three Old Testament prophets are so designated in the superscriptions of their books; the other two are Haggai and Zechariah.

Since such use of the term is rather unusual, we are faced with the question: Is there some special reason for designating Habakkuk a prophet? Is this a way of identifying his status as a professional prophet? In light of the musical nature of chapter 3, was Habakkuk a member of a prophetic guild responsible for temple music (see 1 Chron. 25:1–8)?

Second, the book contains several liturgical features, which we will discuss in detail later. Is the Book of Habakkuk perhaps a liturgy for temple worship, composed by the prophet for some specific occasion of penitence?

Third, chapter 3 contains several musical notations and performance instructions (see, for example, verses 1, 3, and 19). Notice that the last comment of the book reads, "on my stringed instruments." Does this passage suggest a musical role for Habakkuk in temple worship? Did he perhaps accompany himself instrumentally as he led the people in the worship liturgy?

Fourth, legend identifies Habakkuk as a member of the priestly family of Levi. Do the factors above, demonstrating Habakkuk's concern for public worship, lend credibility to this legend? If so, the legend itself becomes yet another piece of evidence to associate Habakkuk with Jerusalem's religious establishment.

Habakkuk may have been a prophet who was part of the

formal worship structure; he may have composed liturgies and hymns for public worship as well as led the people in services at the temple. Though we tend to identify professional prophets as false prophets (because of passages like 1 Kings 22), such was not always the case. Nathan, for example, was a part of David's official court, but his ministry was legitimate. Habakkuk, anointed by God with the spirit of genuine prophecy, likewise may have been within the establishment.

5. Habakkuk's Personality

One cannot help but grasp the intensity of Habakkuk's personality reflected in the three chapters of his book. The autobiographical framework of this material allows us to glimpse into his very being; several characteristics are apparent.

First, Habakkuk was an honest doubter, contemplative and speculative by nature. In a sense he was to the prophets of the Old Testament what Thomas was to the apostles of the New. As a careful observer of life, he could not harmonize the evil he saw around him with his concept of God as good, just, and sovereign. Why did evil seem to have such a free rein? Why did the wicked seem to prevail over the righteous? His questioning spirit simply could not put all of the pieces together.

Second, his doubts stemmed not only from his speculative nature but also from his moral and ethical sensitivity. He was increasingly alarmed by the lawlessness and violence around him. It was not right that evil always seemed to have its way. He hurt not only for those who suffered in Judah but also for those who suffered in other nations (1:17).

Third, Habakkuk searched for truth. He refused to close his eyes to the evil around him. At the same time, he refused to gloss over questions about evil that disturbed him. Instead of letting his anguish and his doubts get the best of him, he faced them honestly, seeking answers from the only One capable of providing them.

Fourth, he maintained profound reverence for God. He knew that God was the only source to answer his questions. In this light, it is striking to examine Habakkuk's questions. They are never directed against God; they are addressed to Him in reverence.

Fifth, Habakkuk was a man with deep personal faith. He did not use his doubts to avoid his relationship with God; rather he turned to God in the midst of his confusion. His consequent struggle produced spiritual growth. The Habakkuk at the end of the book is not the same as the one at the beginning. Early he complains, trying to understand the mysterious ways of God (1:2–4, 12–17). Later he confirms his faith in God unconditionally (3:17–19). Though he does not gain final answers to the questions that trouble him, he realizes anew the loving presence of God. The issue of theodicy must be left in God's hands; regardless of what happens, Habakkuk will trust God. His faith becomes patient and persevering. Even if life's daily provisions are missing, he will trust God. Thus for Habakkuk, God Himself becomes the ultimate source of life and the greatest joy. What a model for victorious living is this prophet!

B. Habakkuk the Book

The Book of Habakkuk is the eighth in the Old Testament minor prophet collection, standing between Nahum and Zephaniah in both the Masoretic text and the LXX. Its acceptance in the canon has been unquestioned by both Christian and Jewish traditions.

1. The Purpose of the Book of Habakkuk

Those who feel Habakkuk's purpose is to describe Babylon's overthrow, as Nahum described Nineveh's, miss the book's point. Habakkuk, instead, is designed to show how a speculative mind can deal with the problem of theodicy and arrive at an answer for living.

From the prophet's struggle come two guidelines for the contemporary reader: (1) It is proper to struggle with life's complexities, to try to understand the problem that the reality of evil presents for faith, to take questions of "Why?" and "How long?" to God. In fact, such struggling doubt reflects a better relationship with God than superficial religious behavior. (2) It is better to live in faith than in rebellion, trusting God when answers are not to be found, living a life of faithfulness even when evil seems to have the upper hand. This approach to life is wise because God is the omnipotent ruler; He will ultimately prevail over evil.

2. The Nature of the Literature in Habakkuk

It is difficult to categorize the literature of Habakkuk. The prophet has done a masterful job of fusing many diverse forms into a literary unit. The book contains elements of poetry,[1] prophecy,[2] wisdom,[3] and liturgy.[4] Habakkuk's framework is yet another literary form—autobiography (see 1:1–3, 12; 2:1–3; 3:1–2, 16–19). But is the book a liturgy composed for formal worship? Or is it a book of wisdom? Or is the book merely an autobiographical account of the prophet's experience? These questions are difficult to answer, and Habakkuk's interpreters hold different opinions about them.

On the other hand, the canonical tradition has identified Habakkuk as prophetic literature by its placement in the book of the twelve prophets. The book's purpose surely serves a prophetic function. Though the framework is Habakkuk's experience and his questions to God, the book ultimately and canonically presents a message from God to believers in troubled times. For them, the prophetic word is to trust God and live in righteousness, even when things are bad. God will prevail.

[1] Poetic elements include: parallelism in 1:8, 1:15, and elsewhere; the evidence of the Qinah measure (see page 23 for definition) in passages like 1:2–3 and 1:5; the hymn in chapter 3; the chiastic structure of the book (the order of words is reversed in two otherwise parallel phrases); and the picturesque imagery, especially in the last chapter.

[2] Prophetic elements include: laments (1:2–4, 12–17); the prophet's dialogue with God (1:2–2:4, which is similar to Jeremiah 1:4–19 and 15:10–21); the foretelling (1:6); and the taunt song and prophetic woes (2:6–20).

[3] Wisdom elements in Habakkuk include the aphorism (a terse saying embodying a general truth) in 2:4, which is reminiscent of the Book of Proverbs; the words of personal affirmation coupled with theophany (manifestation of God), which are similar to passages in Job (compare Hab. 3:2–19 with Job 38:1–42:6); several vocabulary words; and Habakkuk's questioning search for understanding, which reminds one of Job.

[4] Liturgical elements in Habakkuk are many: the word "oracle" in 1:1, which is often used as a technical term for formal curses against foreign enemies; the placement of a lament at the prophecy's beginning in 1:2–4; the liturgical prayer form with elements of complaint and response in 1:2–2:4; the formal character of the instructions to Habakkuk in 2:1–3; the woes in 2:6–20, which could have been a public worship response to the preceding oracle; the word "prayer" in 3:1, which often has liturgical overtones; the musical notations in chapter 3, which were often used with liturgies; and the response of faith at the book's conclusion in 3:17–19.

However, identifying the book's prophetic character does not resolve the issues. Was Habakkuk's prophecy ever used as liturgy in formal services? Perhaps so, especially the hymn in chapter 3 with its musical instructions. But was the Book of Habakkuk actually composed for worship purposes? Perhaps, though the book could be yet another illustration of the literary ability of the Old Testament prophets. These unique and inspired men were able to take many literary forms and use them aptly to proclaim the message from God. The Book of Habakkuk is possibly a prophetic imitation of a liturgy for a worship service, designed to show a believer's struggles which lead to a deeper commitment of faith.

3. Critical Problems in the Book of Habakkuk

Who are the wicked in Habakkuk 1:4 and 1:13? Are they the same in both passages? Is the oppression lamented by Habakkuk within Judah or from without? Who are the recipients of the woes in chapter 2:6–20? The lack of clear answers in the text has led interpreters down many and varied roads.

The traditional view is that the prophet first protests the oppression within Judah; the nation's wicked people were persecuting their fellow Judeans (1:2–4). When Habakkuk questioned God about such tragedy, the divine response was that judgment would come against Judah's wicked community at the hands of the Babylonians (1:5–11).

This response raised an even greater difficulty for Habakkuk. Despite Judah's wickedness, the Babylonians were far worse. How could they be allowed to prevail over those more righteous (1:12–2:1)? Again God answers Habakkuk (2:2–20). Though the answer does not intellectually resolve all difficulties, it produces faith in the prophet (3:1–19).

While the traditional view is certainly the most natural reading of the text, not all interpreters accept it. Countless arguments have been raised against the book's unity, with resultant questions about the authorship and date of the various sections.

Many scholars believe Habakkuk addresses only the problem of external oppression. They suggest various combinations of foreign powers as the wicked in 1:4 and 1:13, the punisher of

1:5–11, and the recipients of the woes in 2:6–20. Babylonians, Assyrians, Egyptians, and even Greeks have been identified in these passages. Each change of identity presents inconsistencies and contradictions that then must be rectified by radical surgery on the text.

For example, if the wicked of 1:2–4 are Babylonians, they would not punish themselves in 1:5–11. It is therefore necessary either to delete 1:5–11 from the book or move it to precede 1:2–4. Others would identify the wicked as Assyrians and thus place 1:5–11 after 2:4 to allow for a "smoother reading." Space does not allow a full treatment of the endless variations suggested for chapters 1 and 2. Needless to say, the chapters' integrity has been severely tested.

The relationship of chapter 3 to the remainder of the book is also called into question. Is the last chapter a composition from some ancient hymnal, added by either Habakkuk or a later editor? Or was it an original part of the book? Those who feel the chapter is a later addition by another editor point to the commentary on Habakkuk found among the Dead Sea Scrolls. That commentary, which interprets Habakkuk 1–2, neither contains nor even mentions chapter 3. The chapter's absence from the commentary in no way settles the issue of its original presence; the commentator may have chosen not to discuss the chapter because its content is different in nature from the previous chapters.

Those commentators who argue against Habakkuk's authorship for chapter 3 point to other factors. Some declare the attitude toward God in the chapter differs dramatically from that in chapters 1 and 2. But does that deny Habakkuk's authorship of chapter 3? Would we not expect the prophet's attitude in the two sections to differ somewhat? In the first part of the book, Habakkuk searches for answers to the problem of theodicy; in the final part, he responds with renewed faith to God's offered solution.

Others say the differences of literary type in the two sections demonstrate different authors. Granted there are literary distinctions, but does that deny Habakkuk's authorship of the entire book? Or does it confirm his experience? In the first two chapters, his faith is sorely tried; he is doubting, wavering, struggling. But in chapter 3 his doubts have been satisfactorily answered. Here he breaks forth in prayer, praise, and joy. He makes a triumphant expression of undaunted faith. Surely necessary psychological and spiritual reasons exist for uniting chapter 3 with the rest of the book.

It seems best to conclude that the Book of Habakkuk is indeed a well-constructed literary unit written by Habakkuk, with the natural reading the proper approach for interpretation. This statement does not preclude the possibility of later editorial revision of a minor nature, nor does it suggest that problems with the traditional interpretation are nonexistent, nor does it mean that the book was all written at one time.[5]

This conclusion also should not be construed to reflect a naïve approach to Habakkuk. This book poses some extremely difficult problems.[6] I certainly am not opposed to any effort to see behind the canonical text to better understand God's message. But we must constantly remember that such effort is to some degree subjective.

In that light, the way some scholars handle Habakkuk illustrates well the excesses of certain biblical critics. Karl Marti, for example, sees the first two chapters as groups of fragments from several messages of diverse authorship and date. He leaves only seven verses to the hand of Habakkuk! Marti and others resort to transposition, emendation, and deletion of sections to the point that the text is literally rewritten. The fact that commentators cannot agree on the proposed placements of sections or the limits of material to excise reveals the highly subjective nature of many such efforts. This subjectivity is dangerous if we desire to affirm the authority of God's Word.

It is best to accept the received text as it stands. Certainly the struggle with textual variants and obscure words is essential. But we do not need to transpose major sections, delete long passages, and arbitrarily emend troublesome words unless we are trying to protect some pet scheme of interpretation.

---

[5] The book is probably the compilation of messages and experiences from a ministry that extended over several years.

[6] The Masoretic text, for example, has not been well preserved; it contains many obscure words and difficult passages. Numerous variants exist between the readings in the LXX and the Hebrew, as well as between the Masoretic text and the Qumran Habakkuk scroll.

The received text of Habakkuk, even with its difficulties, is open to meaningful interpretation. Efforts to change it to afford simpler explanations may in reality distort or negate the very message God intended!

4. Major Theological Themes in the Book of Habakkuk

The great issue with which Habakkuk struggles is theodicy. How could a just and holy God allow evil to exist? How could He remain inactive and silent in the face of brutality, injustice, and atrocious inhumanity? Though intellectual answers for the problem ultimately give way to experiential answers, Habakkuk does in fact learn several significant theological truths.

First, he learns that God and good will inevitably triumph. In chapter 2:3 the divine word to the prophet is: "For the revelation awaits an appointed time; it speaks of the end and will not prove false. Though it linger, wait for it." In other words, history is heading for a certain conclusion. One must not judge matters on the basis of present conditions but rather from the long view, looking to the horizon of the future. In God's good time, justice and right will prevail; evil will be totally defeated. This type of eschatological outlook calls for perseverance and patience. Impatience for immediate answers always leaves confusion. God's people must be a waiting people, living with the certain hope that eternity will clarify the issues, revealing the triumph of right.

Second, Habakkuk learns that evil contains the seed of destruction (2:4–20). Individuals and nations who live in pride, arrogance, and self-sufficiency find in the end these very attitudes are their undoing. Though on occasion evil appears to have the upper hand, it is really filled with death and destruction. It cannot and will not endure in God's moral universe. Its transitory nature is an unalterable fact of history.

Third, the prophet learns that those who are right with God are to live by their faithfulness (2:4). They are to be persons of integrity, honesty, moral steadfastness, and trustworthiness. They are to live in confidence, knowing that even inexplicable matters are in God's hands. They recognize that spiritual values are foundational to human well-being. Though they have problems in this fallen world, more importantly, they have spiritual security. In that light, Habakkuk anticipates some form of permanence for the righteous. Their very character leads to a different destiny than that of the wicked. Thus, the permanent nature of good is another unalterable fact of history.

Fourth, Habakkuk learns that while intellectual answers to the enigmas of history may not be available, God is good and He is enough. Accordingly, His people rejoice in His salvation and strength. They await with confidence the triumphant end, even in the midst of oppression and deprivation (3:17–19). People of such faithfulness realize that life with God is life in the deepest sense. With this realization, they are people of real sensitivity and joy regardless of the circumstances. No matter how much the wicked might have, they really have nothing at all; on the other hand, the righteous are abundantly wealthy even in material poverty. Since the book has an autobiographical structure, Habakkuk serves as an illustration of this righteous person living in faithfulness and joy.

Chapter 5

Habakkuk's Problem of Faith
(Habakkuk 1:1–2:20)

The violent conditions around Habakkuk troubled him. They could not be justified with his theological positions. The God he served was good and just, sovereign and omnipotent, yet wickedness prospered in Judah and the larger world. Evil never seemed to be punished. On the other hand, the righteous were often oppressed. Their virtues were seldom, if ever, rewarded. How could he reconcile these apparent inconsistencies?

Habakkuk's struggle is one that people over the ages have identified with: Why is our world so decimated by crime and corruption? Why is there pain and suffering? Why do we constantly live under the threat of war or in actual conditions of war? Why does injustice frequently reign? Or to put the matter on a personal level, why do things so often go against us?

To seek answers to the disturbing issue of theodicy, Habakkuk entered into a dialogue with God. The first two chapters of his book examine his heartfelt questions and God's responses. This major section is divided into five parts: (A) The Book's Title (1:1); (B) Habakkuk's Initial Inquiry (1:2–4); (C) God's Initial Response (1:5–11); (D) Habakkuk's Second Inquiry (1:12–2:1); and (E) God's Second Response (2:2–20).

A. The Book's Title (1:1)

Habakkuk's work is designated as an "oracle" (Hebrew *maśśā'*). As we saw in the discussion of Nahum, a better translation for *maśśā'* is "burden." Passages where it is found generally carry a negative, ominous tone. Such is the case, to some degree, with Habakkuk. The book contains major discussions of judgment on both the wicked community in Judah and their Babylonian oppressors.

And yet the Book of Habakkuk is more than an announcement of judgment. The prophet is eager to share with his readers an answer for living in the midst of life's complexities and injustices. It is therefore necessary to consider a broader meaning for *maśśā'* in Habakkuk than we did in Nahum. While the connotation of "burden" is still applicable, the *maśśā'* in Habakkuk refers to all of the divine word received by the prophet, regardless of its nature. In that light, *maśśā'* is synonymous with "divine revelation." Thus verse 1 could appropriately read: "The divine revelation that Habakkuk the prophet received."

In that connection, the verb rendered "received" by the NIV is actually the Hebrew word "to see." Habakkuk thus "saw" the *maśśā'*. This verb may be a stereotyped, technical term used to describe the prophet's perception of divine revelation regardless of how that revelation came to him. However, in Habakkuk's case the word just may have a literal connotation. Certainly the theophany in chapter 3 seems visionary. We might, therefore, paraphrase verse 1 as follows: "This is the divine revelation that Habakkuk the prophet saw in a vision."[1]

B. Habakkuk's Initial Inquiry (1:2–4)

Habakkuk initiates his message with an agonizing cry to God (1:2), similar in form to the psalms of lament (see for example Pss. 13 and 74). Judah's society was corrupt. Evil was flaunted openly. The wickedness had continued long and was rooted deeply; it became more apparent with every passing day.

For some time ("How long, O LORD, must I call") Habakkuk had been crying to God for help, but to no avail. As a witness to a conflagration would cry "Fire" as a warning, so Habakkuk had been crying "Violence" to God. He had tried to warn Him of the increasing lawlessness and oppression, of the reckless behavior that characterized Judah. But to date God had ignored the

---

[1] The verb "see" in its noun form means "vision." It is used this way in Habakkuk 2:2–3.

warning. It was not that He failed to hear; He rather failed to act!

The degeneracy, coupled with divine inactivity, was almost more than Habakkuk could bear. Why did there have to be evil in God's world? Why did God make him "look at injustice" (1:3)? Why did evil abound before his very eyes?

But the prophet's greater concern was how a God like Yahweh could "tolerate wrong" (1:3). Why did He not remove it from the face of the earth? After all, He was righteous by nature; His righteousness was undeviating. He could not accept sin. Furthermore, was He not the ruler of the world? Everything Habakkuk knew and believed said to him that God could and would stand in opposition to evil. He would bring judgment against it.

And yet the evil in Judah continued unchecked. Was God too weak to intervene? Too ineffective? Too indifferent? How could He remain so aloof in the face of rampant evil?

Habakkuk simply could not reconcile what was happening around him with his theology. He experienced unbearable tension. His problem was not one of unbelief; his struggle came precisely because he did believe. How could the good God he worshiped not judge the evil of the day?

Because God refused to intervene with judgment, the decadent society was unraveling before Habakkuk's eyes. Destruction, violence, strife, and conflict characterized a culture rapidly disintegrating (1:3).[2] The depravity permeated every aspect of Judah's existence.

The situation was so sordid that the law was "paralyzed" or "chilled" (1:4); it was rendered ineffective by abuse, misuse, or total rejection. With the law thus ignored, justice could never prevail. Court decisions favored the powerful, the rich, and the dishonest. On every hand the righteous were circumvented or stymied by the wicked. Control of society by the wicked meant that justice was always "perverted," twisted, or distorted.

---

[2]The word rendered "destruction," often translated "spoiling," refers to violent treatment causing devastation and ruin, whereas the word "violence" refers to cruel conduct intended to hurt others. The words "strife" and "conflict" refer to disputes and controversies that probably occurred at every level of the national life, from the courts down to individual households.

Habakkuk could have given no more graphic picture of a lawless society than he did in this brief section.

Some commentators interpret "the wicked" in verse 4 to be the Chaldeans or some other foreign power. But it is better to identify them as wicked Judeans. If the book is dated about 600 B.C., this would refer to the wicked King Jehoiakim and the many corrupt people who prospered in his reign. In favor of this internal identification of the wicked are the references to the words "law" (*tôrāh*) and "justice" (*mišpāṭ*) in verse 4. In the Old Testament these terms have definite theological connections with Israel's covenant religion. Their use here points to internal corruption rather than external oppression.

C. God's Initial Response (1:5–11)

The divine response to Habakkuk's initial inquiry leaves the prophet stunned. The righteous God was indeed going to judge Judah's wicked people. In fact, the judgment was imminent; the instrument of punishment was being readied for the task. But amazingly that instrument was none other than the Chaldean or Babylonian empire, which even then was advancing through country after country heading for Judah (1:6). The Babylonians were a "ruthless" (fierce and cruel) and "impetuous" (impulsively violent) people, bent on taking by force that which was not their own.

Even though Habakkuk is staggered by God's announcement, he had been warned. God had introduced the oracle in verse 5 with the words: "Look at the nations and watch—and be utterly amazed. For I am going to do something in your days that you would not believe, even if you were told." The prophet was to observe the international scene for the answer to his inquiry. What he would see would amaze him. In Hebrew the word rendered "amazed" actually occurs twice, in two different verbal forms. It is repeated for emphasis, which the NIV has clearly expressed with the translation "be utterly amazed."

But the prophet was not the only one overwhelmed by the divine message. The plurality of the imperatives in verse 5 means that God was addressing others as well as Habakkuk.[3] In

---

[3] On the basis of a minor textual change, the LXX renders "at the nations" as "you despisers," specifically pointing to the wicked population of Judah. Paul used the LXX translation when he quoted Habakkuk 1:5 in Acts 13:41.

that light, the element of surprise and amazement probably differed from person to person. For example, many of the wicked in Judah lived under a false sense of security. They believed God would never judge them. Were they not, after all, the covenant people? The reality of judgment itself was the point of amazement for them.

For the pro-Egyptian party in Judah, the prediction of Babylonian supremacy was a stunning blow. They had cast their lot with Egypt, and now if Habakkuk was on target, they were doomed.

But for Habakkuk himself, and perhaps for others of Judah's righteous community, the amazement stemmed from the struggle with theodicy. Of course the wickedness in Judah was deserving of nothing less than judgment. Had that not been the contention of the prophet's initial inquiry? But how could God raise up a cruel, pagan power like Babylon to punish Judah? This new concern becomes abundantly clear when Habakkuk voices his second inquiry later in the chapter.

A word is in order here about God "raising up the Babylonians" as the instrument of judgment. God is so great in His sovereignty He is even able to use human sin for His own purpose. That was certainly the case here. Obviously God was not responsible for the violence and cruelty practiced by the Babylonians. He did not inspire these attitudes and actions. Likewise He did not force the Babylonians to assume the role of world conqueror. That was their own goal. In "raising up the Babylonians," God allowed them to do what they themselves wanted to do, but He used it for His purposes.

The vivid description of the Babylonians and their military prowess, begun in verse 6, is amplified in verses 7–11. They are a terrifying people, who constantly provoke fear and dread because of their violent, callous nature (1:7). They consider themselves the creators of law by which everyone else must live. The Babylonians alone were to judge the affairs of humanity, for they acknowledged no higher law. Because the law originated in their own self-centeredness and arrogancy, they alone had rights. Wherever they went, they established their system of justice, which conquered nations broke at their own peril.

In verse 8 Habakkuk uses illustrations from nature to describe the unbelievable speed, the eagerness, the savagery, and the ravenous greed of the Babylonian military operations. The hungry wolf prowling at evening and the vulture swooping down from a great distance to tear and rend a victim graphically picture Babylon's insatiable hunger for conquest. Likewise the rapidity by which Nabopolassar and Nebuchadnezzar built their world empire is forcefully reflected here by the swift horses and the wide-ranging horsemen.

Verse 9 describes the Babylonian goals in life, which were nothing other than violence, destruction, and conquest. These were their greatest pleasure. Accordingly, they swept over the earth like the scorching desert wind, gathering so many prisoners that a count was impossible. Innumerable as grains of sand were the many who suffered at Babylon's hand.

Verse 10 describes the Babylonians' haughty attitude. They made light of the leadership of other nations. Their forces were so strong and capable they invaded fortified cities with little effort. Every opponent was overpowered with terrifying ease; no one could stop the Babylonian drive to world domination. In the path over which their armies passed, only destruction remained. It was as if tornadic winds had come and gone, leaving behind tragic devastation and ruin (1:11).

And yet in this vivid description of a seemingly unstoppable power, one of Habakkuk's great theological themes begins to surface: Evil has within itself the seed of destruction. Babylon will not have the last word after all, for within the empire are self-destructive traits: greed (1:6), cruelty (1:7), arrogance and self-sufficiency (1:7), haughtiness (1:10), and blasphemy (1:11).

The last part of verse 11 is especially instructive as it characterizes the Babylonians as "guilty men, whose own strength is their god." They have deified themselves, their own strength, and their military. By deifying themselves, they have defied God. That is sin's essence. The Babylonians, like the wicked people in Judah, stand guilty before Him. Though they were His instrument in Judah's judgment, the Babylonians too would be judged.

D. Habakkuk's Second Inquiry (1:12–2:1)

Habakkuk begins his second inquiry with a confession of faith. He affirms his confidence in Yahweh, whom he proclaims to be unchanging, everlasting, trustworthy, holy, mighty, and pure (1:12–13a). A personal dimension of faith is reflected as he speaks of "my God" and "my Holy One." His reference to God as "Rock" is an acknowledgment that He is the only legitimate fortress in the present crisis.

Because of Yahweh's trustworthiness and His faithfulness to relationships, the righteous community of which Habakkuk is a part will "not die" (1:12). Do we not have in this section and the one preceding a contrast between the permanence of good and the transitory nature of evil (recall the seed of self-destruction mentioned in the previous discussion)? Is the prophet not also contrasting the reality of God with the unreality of the Babylonian deity mentioned in verse 11?

Yet the confident expression of faith could not disguise the heaviness of Habakkuk's heart. The problem of theodicy still remains; in fact it is even more pressing than before. The judgment on Judah's wicked community, a judgment that Habakkuk approved, and had even sought, was indeed coming. But the message of the earlier revelation was inescapable: Judgment would be at the hand of the treacherous Babylonians. They had been "appointed" by God "to execute judgment"; they were "ordained" as His instrument (1:12).

But that raised a thornier issue for Habakkuk. How could God's use of so wicked a nation ever be reconciled with His absolute holiness? If He could never "look" favorably "on evil," how could He ever "tolerate the treacherous" (1:13)?[4] How could He remain "silent" and inactive while the Babylonians swallowed up "those more righteous than themselves" (1:13)?

Because of God's inactivity, the Babylonians' victims had become disorganized, leaderless, and helpless. They were totally incapable of defending themselves. In typical Old Testament fashion, Habakkuk looks beyond any secondary cause for their defenseless condition. It was God Himself who "made" them "like fish" (1:14).

---

[4]The Hebrew verb translated "look" does not simply mean "to gaze upon," but rather "to look with favor." Habakkuk does not mean that God does not see evil; He sees it—but He never favors or accepts it.

Continuing with the same imagery, Habakkuk describes the Babylonians' use of hooks, nets, and dragnets to catch their victims (1:15). These three items symbolize all the weapons and devices used by these savage people to take captives and subdue nations.

The Babylonians' pleasure in their military endeavors was intense (1:15); after all, their numerous conquests had made them wealthy and fat (1:16). They did not recognize God's hand in their many victories; consequently they offered sacrifices and burned incense to the implements to which they attributed their success (1:16). No historical evidence exists to show that the Babylonians literally worshiped their instruments of war; Habakkuk's statement is figurative. The Babylonians really paid homage to themselves and their own brute strength (see verse 11).

In light of such impiety, Habakkuk, with poignant expectation, raises a final question: "Is he to keep on emptying his net, destroying nations without mercy?" (1:17). How long will this cruelty be allowed to continue?

George Adam Smith summarizes well Habakkuk's dilemma of faith:

> In itself such impiety is gross enough, but to a heart that believes in God it is a problem of exquisite pain. Habakkuk's is the burden of the finest faith. He illustrates the great commonplace of religious doubt, that problems arise and become rigorous in proportion to the purity and tenderness of a man's conception of God. It is not the coarsest but the finest temperaments which are exposed to scepticism. Every advance in assurance of God or in appreciation of His character develops new perplexities in face of the facts of experience, and faith becomes her own most cruel troubler.[5]

Having bared his innermost being before God, Habakkuk realizes he can go no further. His alternatives now are two: he can allow his doubts to be either destructive or creative. He can use his doubts, struggles, and agonizing questions to turn from God and to renounce his faith. Or he can keep his hold on God, trusting Him for an answer.

---

[5]George Adam Smith, *The Book of the Twelve Prophets* (New York: Funk & Wagnalls Company, 1900), Vol. 2, p. 136.

Habakkuk's choice of direction is clearly defined in chapter 2:1. He was a man of profound faith, and his struggles gave depth to that faith. Verse 1 describes his turning to God in a spirit of reverence and confident expectation, waiting for the divine answer to the problem.

Commentators debate the exact nature of Habakkuk's action here. Did he go to some isolated tower or height to wait for God to speak? Some believe he had a watch post on the city wall or in an open field. Or is verse 1 figurative? Does it mean that Habakkuk prepared himself mentally and spiritually to receive God's message? The answer is not certain and really is of little importance. The point is that Habakkuk now was willing to leave his problem with God and await the divine response. He was sure God would speak, though he had no idea of the time or the manner. He could only be ready and wait patiently. When God spoke to him, he could then share the answer with others.

E. God's Second Response (2:2–20)

For many people, expressions of doubt are signs of unbelief. But this conclusion is erroneous. Doubts can express a maturing faith. Certainly that is so in Habakkuk's case. As we have seen, the prophet had doubts about how God governed the world, but his faith, while deeply troubled, was never forfeited; it rather grew in the struggle.

Obviously God was in no way unhappy with Habakkuk's persistent questioning. Indeed by responding to him, God endorsed the kind of struggle exemplified in the prophet's life.

Whether the second divine answer came soon or after a long delay, we are not told. Regardless, it was worth any wait. Two of the great passages of the Old Testament—2:4 and 2:20—are found here. The response can be divided into three parts: (1) The Instructions to the Prophet (2:2–3); (2) The Message of the Vision (2:4–5); and (3) The Taunt of the Oppressed (2:6–20).

1. The Instructions to the Prophet (2:2–3)

God's response to Habakkuk's question came in the form of a vision, called "the revelation" in the NIV. Exactly what constitutes the vision is not clear. Some interpreters suggest the message is found in Habakkuk 2:3–4, while others have opted for 2:4 alone or 2:4–5. Because the vision was to be recorded on tablets rather than a single tablet, some expand it to include 2:3–20 or even 2:3–3:19. Others who see disunity in the Habakkuk text identify 1:5–11 as the vision. Julius Bewer takes the word "vision" literally; since the theophany of chapter 3 appears to be the only possible vision in the book (though some question its visionary character), he identifies it as the subject of 2:2.

If the brevity of the written messages in Isaiah 8:1 and 30:7–8 provides any clue for us here, perhaps we should consider 2:4–5 as the message Habakkuk originally wrote on the tablets. The present text, then, is an expansion to include explanatory material like the woes in 2:6–20.

God's first instruction to Habakkuk was to write the vision on tablets (2:2). The word used here for "tablets" is the same one used in connection with the law at Sinai in Exodus 24:12. Commentators debate whether the tablets were of clay, stone, or wood. They also differ about whether the tablets were to be displayed in a public area like the marketplace. Regardless of these issues, the writing of the message was to make it accessible to everyone.

The second instruction was that the vision was to be made "plain" (2:2). Should the verb here be taken literally? Does it mean that the vision was to be written in large, clear-cut, easily read letters? No, it probably means that the message of the vision was to be clearly written so that anyone could easily understand it.

One reason for writing the message was that it could serve as a guide for living, as the NIV marginal reading says, "so that whoever reads it may run with it" (2:2). The Hebrew here clearly puts the emphasis on the running of the reader, not the reading of the runner.

Unfortunately many commentaries reverse Habakkuk's emphasis. By putting the emphasis on the reading of the runner, they interpret the statement to mean that the vision is written in such large, clear letters that a runner, hurrying by, can glance at it and make sense of the message.

But that is not what the Hebrew is saying. It rather means

that the person who reads the message will adopt it as a guide for living; that is, the person will run (similar to the biblical concept of "walk") through life according to it. The NIV textual reading—"so that a herald may run with it"—offers a related interpretation. Here the person who receives (or understands) the message shares it with others ("runs with it").

Another reason for writing the vision was to preserve it until its fulfillment could be demonstrated historically (2:3). The events predicted in the vision would be satisfactorily consummated, but in God's good time ("the revelation awaits an appointed time"). The fulfillment would come in "the end" and would be exactly as God intended ("will not prove false"). The end here may refer to the termination of Babylonian power but, more likely, to the eschaton (the glorious future envisioned by the Old Testament prophets; see the note on page 150).

The last part of verse 3, "it will certainly come and will not delay," merits comment. A superficial reading can lead to misunderstanding. It does not mean that the future events predicted in the vision will come soon, without delay. Only God knows the time for such events. The comment rather means that the fulfillment will not miss God's scheduled time; it will not delay a moment beyond its appointed time.

A significant shift in the book occurs in these verses. Before this the emphasis has been on Habakkuk questioning the way God runs the world. Now the emphasis changes to how people are to live until God's appointed time is realized. The divine word here is that God's people are to wait patiently in faith for fulfillment, which is certain ("though it linger, wait for it; it will certainly come").

2. The Message of the Vision (2:4–5)

The message revealed to Habakkuk did not precisely answer his questions. Nothing was said, for example, about why "the wicked swallow up those more righteous than themselves" (1:13). No immediate relief to the Babylonian terror was promised. And yet as Donald E. Gowan says, "For those who can accept it as God's kind of answer (rather than our own kind) it is answer enough."[6]

The basic message, stated as a general aphorism or saying in verse 4, is this: There are two classes of people in the world; they have distinct moral characters that lead them to different destinies. On the one hand, there are the wicked. They are characterized by pride ("puffed up"), arrogance, and presumption. They do not follow the path of integrity ("are not upright"). Their lives are lived in slavery to self-destructive addictions (see verse 5, "wine betrays him"). Their greed is insatiable, driving them to take by force that which is not theirs ("he is as greedy as the grave and like death is never satisfied, he gathers to himself all the nations and takes captive all the peoples"). The wicked may prevail for a time, but in "the end" (see verse 3), they will perish. Their ultimate destiny is death.

On the other hand, there are the righteous, identified by a Hebrew statement that literally reads, "but the righteous by his faithfulness will live"(2:4b). These people live in right relationship with God. The concept "live" is pregnant with meaning. It refers to life in the light of divine favor and approval; such life may not always bring material prosperity, but it brings fullness, moral security, and meaning. Such life is lived on the basis of faithfulness. The word rendered "faith" in 2:4 is the Hebrew 'emûnāh, which literally means "faithfulness." In other words, the righteous are themselves reliable, trustworthy, and dependable.

This brief section presents several textual problems. The first six Hebrew words of verse 4 and the first eight words of verse 5 are difficult to translate. Though many commentators have given up hope of precise translations, we can be confident that our various English versions have captured the passage's basic essence.

Two of the textual problems deserve brief consideration. First, no subject is identified at the outset of verse 4. Who is the "he" who is puffed up? Both wicked Judeans and Babylonians, as well as other foreign powers, have been suggested. Some commentators propose textual additions like "the oppressor," "the unjust," and "the evildoer."

[6] Donald E. Gowan, *The Triumph of Faith in Habakkuk* (Atlanta: John Knox Press, 1976), p. 41.

But is there really a problem here? It is evident that the verse draws a contrast between the righteous (who are specifically identified) and the "he." In that light, could not "he" simply be identified as any who are not righteous, who do not live by faithfulness? While the Babylonians might have been the most evident example of that class in Habakkuk's day, is not the passage broad enough to identify all "puffed up" persons who oppose God and worship themselves?

Second, while 2:4 clearly states the righteous will live, it does not clarify the wicked's fate. Perhaps the matter did not need formal statement. Again the obvious contrast drawn in the verse permits the view that if the righteous live, the wicked die. Likewise the implication of death may have a more powerful literary effect than an explicit comment.

At the same time commentators offer several legitimate interpretations that may solve the difficulty. Some read "his desires are not upright" as "his life is not stable or not straight," which would indicate a negative end. The phrase "never at rest" in verse 5 could mean "he will not survive" or "he will not be successful."

J. A. Emerton bases an interesting interpretation on the verb "to fly," which he finds in the text by dividing a word already there into two separate words. His reading sees the life that is not upright as flying away or perishing.[7] Any one of these suggestions or several in combination solve the matter of the wicked's fate.

Note here that Habakkuk 2:4b played a pivotal role in the development of Paul's doctrine of justification by faith (see Rom. 1:17; Gal. 3:11) and, through Paul, influenced Martin Luther and the Protestant Reformation. Commentators have gone to great lengths to stress the difference between Habakkuk's concept of "faithfulness" and Paul's concept of "faith." Paul, on the one hand, declares that eternal salvation is provided for those who are justified by their faith-response to God's grace in Christ. People are not saved by their good works but by trustful reliance on the Lord. Habakkuk, on the other hand, indicates that righteous people are themselves faithful and dependable,

---

[7] J. A. Emerton, "The Textual and Linguistic Problems of Habakkuk II. 4–5," *Journal of Theological Studies* 28 (1977):16–17.

that is, they are people of integrity, living by loyalty to the covenant and Yahweh's revealed will.

Though distinctions do exist, perhaps they are not as great as we have made them. Does not Paul's position leave room for justified persons to live their daily Christian experience in loyalty and fidelity to God's revealed will? Do his comments not allow for personal faithfulness? Do not Habakkuk's righteous persons live their lives of faithfulness because they are committed by faith to God? Their faithfulness surely must be lived in relationship with something! Is not the Old Testament emphasis on a relationship with God?

One scholar explained the difference between Paul and Habakkuk with the assertion that Paul talked about trusting a person. Did not Habakkuk consider God a person to be trusted? Why else would one live in faithfulness to Him? Gowan concludes this matter well when he states: "In the Bible there is no ground for separating faith, what one believes, from faithfulness, how one behaves."[8]

The message of Habakkuk's vision boils down to this: In "the end" the destinies of the wicked and the righteous will be evident. One will perish and the other will live. Though this may not be apparent today, "it will certainly come." Evil has within itself the seed of destruction, and in time it will perish; righteousness, however, has within itself endurance and permanence. The prophet was thus admonished to live his life in daily faithfulness, trusting that history's final outcome was in God's hand. A life of faithfulness is to be the response to life's many unanswered questions.

3. The Taunt of the Oppressed (2:6–20)

This section expands Habakkuk 2:4a. It declares that the wicked, in God's moral providence, are doomed. Evil's inherent tendency is to self-destruct. The vices of the wicked carry within them their own just reward. Accordingly, the judgment, which Habakkuk felt so theologically necessary, was to be a reality. God was indeed in control of the world.

The passage is composed of five woe oracles. Each woe

---

[8] Gowan, *Triumph of Faith*, p. 43.

both identifies a particular sin of the wicked and announces, either explicitly or implicitly, retribution. The Hebrew participial form is used throughout this section, indicating that the various sins were the continual habits and practices of the wicked.

A major critical problem in this section is the speakers' identity. Though we have included the passage in God's second response to Habakkuk, note that the words of the taunt song are actually placed in the mouth of "all of them" (2:6). To whom does this ambiguous phrase apply?

Many commentators see "the nations" and "the peoples" of verse 5 as the antecedent. While this view fits grammatically, does it make sense? Would pagan nations condemn idolatry (as they do in the final woe)? Other commentators identify "all of them" as Habakkuk and the righteous community.

Perhaps we should not make too much of the speakers' identity. Certainly our inability to make a precise identification in no way negates the section's purpose. It expands the negative dimension of the general aphorism in verse 4: While the righteous live, the wicked die. Therefore though God is not identified as the speaker of 2:6–20, the passage continues His earlier thought and is legitimately included in His second response to Habakkuk.

Another difficult issue is the identity of the wicked whose doom is pronounced by the woes. It is not said that they are the wicked from Babylonia or Judah, though both would certainly be applicable to Habakkuk's day. Perhaps the passage is not specific because it applies to the wicked of any age, even our own.

The comment "taunt him with ridicule and scorn" in verse 6 contains three important Hebrew words. The first one is generally translated "proverb" or "parable," though here it means a derisive poem or taunt song. The other two words can be translated "scornful riddles," "taunting proverbs," or "mocking enigmas." Since Habakkuk uses these words to describe the content of 2:6–20, it is not surprising to find in the section terms that have an enigmatic character and dual meaning.

The first woe is against those of insatiable greed (2:6–8). They steal, extort, and plunder, using every device they can imagine to take what does not belong to them. But what they have done will one day be done to them.

In verse 7 the word translated "debtors" can also mean "biters." It is used in the latter sense for a serpent's bite (see Gen. 49:17). Therefore it serves as a double entendre here (a word with a double meaning). The victims of the wicked are "debtors," but they will suddenly become "biters." One day they will rise up, making the wicked "tremble," or "shake violently," and pay them back in kind for the agony received at their hand. Verse 8 illustrates well the biblical principle that what people sow they also reap (see Gal. 6:7).

The second woe is against those who build their house (or "realm" or dynasty) by exploiting others (2:9–11). Condemned here are not only acts of exploitation but also the attitudes of covetousness from which they come. Such self-centered people seek to make their strongholds impregnable ("to set his nest on high") and themselves inaccessible to calamity ("to escape the clutches of ruin").

However, by stepping on others, they in reality ruin themselves (2:10). The shameful means taken to secure stability and status guarantee ruin; the overthrow of others eventually brings retribution. Here is a striking example both of evil's inherent tendency to self-destruct and of wickedness being repaid measure for measure (see Isa. 33:1).

Verse 11 contains a striking personification. The house's stones, secured by exploitation, will cry out in protest against the injustices. Their indictment of the wicked will be seconded in antiphonic response by the beams or rafters of the house.

The third woe is against those who attempt to create society by means of violence and tyranny (2:12–14). Habakkuk obviously had in mind military conquest and political assassination. Perhaps he also meant human sacrifice (see 1 Kings 16:34). Certainly forced labor is indicated by verse 13.

But the woe also has individual implications. People build their own small domains within society's larger structures, often through injustice and corruption. Society built in this manner will not last. It is doomed to destruction ("for the fire") because it is in reality "nothing" or "empty" (2:13). Such societies are transitory because they stand in opposition to God's kingdom, which even now is being brought to fulfillment. Inevitably His kingdom will prevail; as universal sovereign, His glory will be recognized across the earth (2:14). What a contrast between His reign and the nothingness of iniquitous societies!

This woe sees judgment more as God's direct intervention whereas the first two emphasize the processes of decay and retribution within evil itself. Here God determines the destruction of sinful societies (2:13). It is "the LORD Almighty" who brings in His own kingdom.

This section clearly demonstrates the influence of earlier prophets on Habakkuk. Verse 12 is related to Micah 3:10, while verse 14 is a slightly altered quote from Isaiah 11:9. Verse 13 and Jeremiah 51:58 are clearly related, but who influenced whom is not clear since these prophets were contemporaries.

The fourth woe is against those who are guilty of inhumanity (2:15–17). They delight in degrading others, in using them for their own amusement. Accordingly, they intoxicate their neighbors to lead them into perversion (2:15). Most commentators interpret this passage figuratively, referring to national powers (such as Babylon) humiliating captive people by stripping them of their independence, dignity, and honor. Habakkuk's words are surely applicable to both individual and corporate situations.

The wicked will experience an overwhelming dose of the same medicine (2:16). Rather than bringing them "glory," honor, or a good reputation, their actions will eventually fill them with "shame." "Disgrace will cover" their "glory," ruining their reputations. They will be forced by God's hand to experience the drunkenness and exposure they forced on others. Once again people will reap what they have sown.

Two matters in verse 16 are especially striking. First, the NIV contains the statement: "drink and be exposed!" The Hebrew text literally reads: "Drink you also and show yourself uncircumcised" or "Drink you also and uncover your foreskin!" Many of the ancient versions, including the Qumran Habakkuk scroll and the LXX, transpose two letters in the relevant Hebrew word and read "stagger or reel" (see the NIV margin). This variant reading makes good sense in the context ("drink and stagger"). However, is it not possible Habakkuk was referring here to the wicked's uncircumcision as an evidence that they were not God's people? If so, the reading "drink and show yourself uncircumcised" (which parallels "naked bodies" in verse 15) is preferred.

Second, the word rendered "disgrace" can be construed as a combination of two Hebrew words, the one meaning "vomit, spew" and the other meaning "shame, disgrace." The combination would read "shameful vomiting." If this reading is adopted, we have here another of Habakkuk's double entendres. On the one hand, the word is a strong term for disgrace, that is, "extreme disgrace"; on the other hand, the word refers to vomiting caused by excessive drinking, which fits the context well. To say it another way, Habakkuk's special word emphasizes the extreme disgrace that comes to the wicked, while at the same time portraying the tragic scene of persons totally depraved, lying in their own vomit.

The violence mentioned in verse 17 is reminiscent of the earlier woes, leading some commentators to believe the passage is out of place here. The historical allusion to Lebanon's destruction cannot be precisely identified. Is it perhaps a reference to the location of Babylon's army at the time Habakkuk was writing? Though we cannot answer that question, the theme of the verse is clear. The wicked not only destroy people, but they also rape and ravage nature, destroying Lebanon's beautiful cedar forests and the animals that live there. For such abusive action against the creation there will be a sure retribution.

The fifth woe is against those who are guilty of idolatry (2:18–20). Unlike the other passages in this section, the final oracle does not begin with the word "woe." It begins instead with an ironic rhetorical question, which evaluates negatively the worth of idols (2:18).

The "woe" appears at the outset of verse 19, prompting some interpreters to transpose the oracle's first two verses. Such a change, however, negates the unique role of the final woe. By the slightly altered arrangement, Habakkuk tries to draw attention to these three verses. They are designed, first, to emphasize the wicked's root problem (that they reject the true God to serve false gods) and second, to prepare the way for the theophany (or manifestation of God) in chapter 3.

The oracle depicts the absurdity of idolatry. The idols are called in Hebrew *'elîlîm*. This word means "nongods" or "nonentities." Whereas some people in ancient Israel believed gods other than Yahweh existed, the prophets witnessed passionately to the existence of Yahweh alone. The use of a word like *'elîlîm* is a strong argument for this case. The word was evidently first used, perhaps even coined, by the prophet Isaiah.

Habakkuk's description of the idols in 2:18–19 underscores the folly of worshiping them. They are limited by the very limitations of the people who make them. They teach lies in that their presence deludes the unsuspecting into believing they can act. But in reality they cannot speak, see, hear, think, move, or "give guidance." How could they possibly save or meet some human need? Though they are beautifully adorned "with gold and silver," they are totally lifeless ("no breath") and consequently are totally useless.

In stark contrast to the idols' impotence is Yahweh's omnipotence (2:20). He is the righteous, universal ruler, residing in His heavenly temple (see Ps. 11:4–7). Whereas idols deserve no respect or consideration, Yahweh demands universal submission and solemn silence. Before Him all the earth is to stand in hushed expectancy and awed reverence, awaiting His judicial announcement.

Verse 20 rings with finality. The moral God is on His throne. It is His government that controls the world. The righteous stand before Him in the permanence of their faithfulness. The wicked, who have rejected Him for "nongods," face their terrible destiny. Habakkuk had found at last a viable solution for his problem of faith.

Chapter 6

Habakkuk's Response of Faith
(Habakkuk 3:1–19)

The debate about the relationship of Habakkuk 3 to the rest of the book remains a major issue in Old Testament studies. Why do we have a new title in chapter 3:1? Does its presence prove chapter 3 was not originally part of the book? Why did the Qumran Habakkuk commentary fail to include chapter 3? Did Habakkuk borrow this chapter's content from some ancient hymnal? Did some later editor append chapter 3 to Habakkuk's book because its authorship was ascribed to Habakkuk?

Regardless of the answers we give, the foundational position is this: As the Book of Habakkuk now stands in the canon, chapter 3 is the necessary conclusion to the prophet's experience. He had approached God with the problem of his faith. He had agonized over the issue of theodicy. And God had answered him—not once, but twice.

Of course the divine response did not address all of the intellectual issues the prophet raises. Habakkuk still did not understand why evil had to exist in God's good universe. He still did not know why the wicked so often prevailed over the good. But now he knew that the righteous live by their faithfulness and that the wicked eventually perish. He knew that in the future God's purposes would be ultimately fulfilled.

What would be Habakkuk's response to the divine revelation? In chapter 3 we learn it was a response of profound faith. The chapter is thus a remarkable and fitting conclusion to the book.

Chapter 3 divides into three parts: (A) Habakkuk's Prayer

(3:1–2); (B) God's Manifestation (3:3–15); and (C) Faith's Victory (3:16–19).

A. Habakkuk's Prayer (3:1–2)

Habakkuk responds to God with a confession of faith, identified in the chapter title as a "prayer" (3:1). An untranslatable phrase—"on *shigionoth*"—is also included in the title.

Etymological studies, attempting to define the word *shigionoth*, have been fraught with difficulties. Most scholars consider it a technical, musical term, indicating perhaps the hymn tune by which the prayer was to be sung or the type of music by which it was to be accompanied. The additions of the technical term *selah* (3:3, 9, 13) and the instruction at the book's end (3:19) make it evident that chapter 3 was used in public worship.[1] Whether it was used as a separate piece or in combination with chapters 1 and 2 as a liturgy is open to question.

The prayer begins in verse 2, appropriately enough, with the divine name "Yahweh," by which the ancient Judeans knew God's covenant faithfulness. Habakkuk's use of the name reflects his attitude of humility as well as his spirit of trust. Various elements common to prayer are included here: (1) praise ("I have heard of your fame"); (2) adoration ("I stand in awe"); (3) a reflection on God's nature and acts ("your fame," "your deeds"); and (4) petition ("renew them," "in wrath remember mercy").

The phrase rendered "your fame" literally reads "your report" in Hebrew. Some commentators associate the "report" specifically with the divine responses in chapters 1 and 2. Others feel Habakkuk was thinking back to distant events of God's saving action, perhaps the Exodus. There is nothing to eliminate either possibility and, in fact, the combination of both past and present revelations makes better sense. Habakkuk had come to his crisis of faith with a knowledge about God; this had been magnified during the struggle recorded in the book.

But whatever the precise content of the report, it left Habakkuk "in awe." Was his awe or fear a terror about the

---

[1] The word *selah* has an uncertain meaning. It may be an instruction for instrumental accompaniment or a change of tempo.

coming judgment at Babylon's hand? So some believe. But is it not better to see the awe as an expression of Habakkuk's reverence and respect for God?

The earlier dialogue with God had reinforced Habakkuk's own view that judgment must come, but it had also given him an even greater perception of the God he served. From a human perspective, he experienced some fear at the impending Babylonian invasion. But he also felt greater awe and more profound respect for God, the universal judge, who resided in His heavenly temple looking down at sinful humanity.

Habakkuk's prayer contains two specific petitions. First, reflecting on God's saving actions in history, the prophet implores: "Renew them in our day." Emphatically he repeats the request: "In our time make them known."

Some writers criticize Habakkuk at this point, believing his impatient attitude from the earlier dialogue resurfaces here (see 1:2). But that does not appear to be the case. His "How long?" was indeed an impatient cry. But his "Renew them in our day" is a positive expression of longing faith and bold hope. The tone of his petition is similar to that of the later writer who cried: "Amen. Come, Lord Jesus" (Rev. 22:20).

Habakkuk's second petition to God is "in wrath remember mercy." He does not ask to be spared from the approaching conflict, nor does he pray that God would keep Judah from war with Babylon. He knew these things were to be—indeed, had to be. He likewise does not ask God to remember the merits of the righteous; he rather asks God to remember Himself, His own nature. Habakkuk therefore pleads that God temper the judgment with mercy.

B. God's Manifestation (3:3–15)

The remarkable theophany, or manifestation of God, in these verses forms the heart of chapter 3. This section might be a continuation of Habakkuk's prayer in which he reflects on what he knows of God. Or perhaps Habakkuk received here a vision of a future theophany in which God would redeem His people. Or maybe these verses are a combination of the two. Did Habakkuk receive a vision of a future theophany, a vision that was radically colored by his awareness of God's past acts?

A major reason for the difficulty here is that the Hebrew verbs could be rendered as past, present, or future tense. Is Habakkuk considering God's past saving actions and praying for their repetition in his day? Or is he envisioning a future redemption for God's people? Or is he comprehending a revelation of God's constancy, describing what God is always doing in His government of the world?

No dogmatic answers can be given to any of these questions. But it is necessary to recognize that this section contains several points of contact with Israel's history, particularly the Exodus-Sinai event. Yet the passage appears to be more than mere historical reflection on Habakkuk's part. He responds to the revelation like an overwhelmed person (see 3:16). Therefore it would be unwise to rule out arbitrarily a visionary experience.

It would appear that, in one sense, the passage continues Habakkuk's prayer, reflecting on what God has done in the hope of what He will do. But it would also seem that the theophanic experience that follows the prayer is indeed a vision that shook Habakkuk to his core. With the use of vivid poetic imagery and historical allusion, yet with profound originality, he attempts to describe for his readers what he was privileged to see.

This highly significant passage is divided into three parts: (1) The Theophany's Description (3:3–7); (2) Habakkuk's Questions (3:8–11); and finally (3) The Theophany's Meaning (3:12–15).

1. The Theophany's Description (3:3–7)

As Habakkuk continued to pray, he saw God coming like a warrior from Teman and Mount Paran (3:3). Teman as a proper name refers to a district in the northern part of Edom; as a common noun it means "the south." Paran is the mountainous area west of the Gulf of Aqabah, near the traditional location of Mount Sinai. These regions to the south of Judah evoked strong memories of the Exodus. Note that God is seen coming from His ancient dwelling place rather than from Jerusalem (as one would expect in Habakkuk's day). These geographical references in the theophanic experience serve as the first point of contact with Israel's history.

As God moved northward, the entire southern horizon was

covered by His "glory" or radiance; His majestic brilliance spread across the skies (3:3). "His praise filled the earth." This statement does not mean that human praise to God could be heard from everywhere; it rather means that God's revelation demonstrated His worthiness to be praised. A secondary meaning of the Hebrew word might also be in the prophet's mind; the word translated "praise" can also mean "splendor."

The initial line of verse 4 in the Hebrew text differs from that in the NIV. The NIV reads: "His splendor was like the sunrise," whereas the Hebrew declares: "And brightness was as the light." Though the reading is difficult, its meaning is clear: as God advanced, His appearance was like an intense, brilliant light. "Rays flashed from his hand." The imagery here may be that of lightning or, more likely, sun rays. If lightning is the image, we have another allusion to the Exodus-Sinai event (see Exod. 19:16).

The brilliance of the theophany was such that one would have thought it sufficient to reveal God and His power. But it was so blinding it served instead to hide or veil Him ("his power was hidden"). Even in God's revelations there is hiddenness; He manifests Himself yet remains invisible and concealed.

As the theophany continued, plague and pestilence accompanied God on His journey (3:5). These are remarkable personifications. The word "plague" is the Hebrew *debher*. As a common noun, it can mean "disease," "plague," "catastrophe," or "death." The word "pestilence" (Hebrew *resheph*) can be translated "fiery bolts," "burning heat," "flames," and "lightnings." Interpreted simply as common nouns here, the first word refers to the plague that comes in Yahweh's wake while the second word refers to the fever that accompanies such sickness. There is probably an allusion here to the pestilence in Egypt at the time of the Exodus.

The two words may be seen, however, from another perspective. Several scholars contend that "Debher" and "Resheph" were the names of specific demons who, in this passage, served as God's bodyguards or attendants in warfare. Archaeology has discovered in the ancient Near Eastern world a demon-god of pestilence named Resheph; similar evidence for Debher is also thought to exist. However, it is mere speculation that Habakkuk understood Debher and Resheph to be demonic beings. It is much more likely that he used these words as common nouns, personified by poetry.

One other possibility does exist. If Habakkuk did understand them as demonic beings, the passage may have a different interpretation. Rather than accompanying God, Debher and Resheph instead hurried out of His way as He continued to His destination.

In verse 6 God took His stand on the earth. The NIV, adopting a variant reading, states: "He stood, and shook the earth." The Hebrew literally reads: "He stood and measured earth." With the discerning eye of the righteous judge, He surveyed the world. His penetrating look "made the nations tremble" in fear of His wrath. His awesome presence caused havoc in the earth itself. Mountains that had stood for centuries "crumbled" under Him. "Age-old hills," symbols of stability and permanence, "collapsed."

Among the nations that trembled at the divine presence were the desert tribes of Cushan and Midian (3:7). Habakkuk witnessed their terror, which was reminiscent of the terror of the various peoples at the Exodus (see Exod. 15:14–16).

The word "Cushan" occurs only here in the Old Testament. Though some consider it a lengthened spelling of Cush, and thus a reference to Ethiopia or Egypt, most recognize here a kindred tribe of the Midianites or perhaps even a Midianite branch. Mention of Midian, of course, is a certain reminder of Israel's Exodus-Sinai experience (see Exod. 2:15–22).

2. *Habakkuk's Questions* (3:8–11)

In this section Habakkuk abruptly shifts from third to second person narrative. Interrupting the theophanic description, he addresses God. The prophet is puzzled. Therefore he asks a series of questions designed to uncover the purpose of the divine manifestation (3:8). Why had God come riding with His horses and chariots? Was He angry with the rivers, streams, and sea?

Before an answer is given, a fierce battle is graphically described (3:9–11). God the mighty warrior was well prepared for this combat. He moved against His enemies with bow (3:9), arrows (3:9, 11), and "flashing spear" (3:11). The effect was devastating. The mountains "writhed" as if in great pain (3:10). "The deep roared" like a person in anguish (3:10); it "lifted its waves on high," like a person gesturing in distress. The "sun and moon stood still in the heavens" (3:11).

The passage is filled with vivid imagery. Was a great thunderstorm behind Habakkuk's presentation? Does a thunderstorm with its lightning and torrential rains explain a statement like "you split the earth with rivers" (3:9) and "torrents of water swept by" (3:10)? Were God's arrows and spear the flashes of lightning? Were the sun and moon ineffective because they were hidden behind dark clouds or eclipsed by the brilliant display of lightning? Were Yahweh's horses and chariots the storm clouds and hurricane winds?

Or were other natural occurrences behind the prophet's picture? Was an earthquake responsible for the trembling of the mountains (3:10)? Did such a cataclysm create the new channels for the rivers (3:9)? Is the phenomenon of eclipse behind verse 11?

Do images from nature necessarily exhaust Habakkuk's resource material? Could the horses and chariots perhaps be an allusion to angelic beings? Or are they simply figurative expressions relevant to the military scene poetically described here?

The passage is likewise replete with historical allusion. Certainly Yahweh's victory over the waters is reminiscent of those earlier mighty acts at the great sea (Exod. 14:15–31; 15:1–21) and the Jordan River (Josh. 3:9–4:18). The writhing of the mountains may reflect the earthquake of the Sinai experience (Exod. 19:18). The flood story may be behind verse 10. Some commentators suggest the famous event in Joshua's life (Josh. 10:12–14) as the basis for the sun and moon standing still in verse 11. If so, Habakkuk uses the language of that miracle but changes the idea. There the luminaries remained active so that Joshua would have more light for the battle; here they are darkened by God's radiance.

We cannot be certain of all the imagery and historical allusion that influenced the prophet's mind, both as he witnessed the theophany and as he attempted to describe it. He obviously developed a composite of images that he used creatively in an effort to share his theophanic experience. Our attempts to decipher the various images in a passage like this often distract from the overall effect. The passage is impressive, picturesque, and meaningful as it stands. Perhaps it would be better to experience it rather than analyze it. The passage strikes our senses in a powerful way. Its remarkable picture of the warrior God overwhelms us if we open ourselves to it. Was this not perhaps Habakkuk's original purpose for the presentation?

3. The Theophany's Meaning (3:12–15)

Habakkuk's questions in verse 8 are answered in the final section of the theophanic experience. Why had God come? It was not because He was angry with the waters. He had come "in wrath," first, to judge the "nations" (3:12) and second, to save His people and the "anointed one" (3:13). We are immediately reminded of the truth that dominates this book: The wicked will perish, "but the righteous will live by his faith" (2:4).

Several points in this section merit brief consideration. First, the prophet says in 3:12 that God "threshed the nations." The Hebrew verb also offers the translations "to tread" or "to trample." The imagery is highly significant. In Habakkuk's day oxen were used to thresh wheat and corn. They would tread on it or trample it, separating the grain from the stalk. Similarly, God threshes the nations, separating the righteous from the wicked.

Second, various people have identified the "anointed one" (3:13) as the Messiah, the Davidic king, the high priest, and the Israelites. The latter interpretation suits the context well; it allows Habakkuk 3:13b to parallel 3:13a. However the reference is probably best understood as the Davidic king.

Third, the last half of 3:13 in the NIV reads: "You crushed the leader of the land of wickedness, you stripped him from head to foot." The Hebrew literally states: "You struck [shattered] the head from the house of the wicked, laying bare the foundation to the neck." Habakkuk either mixes his metaphors here (head of house; neck of person), or more likely, he figuratively uses the house to represent a person. The sense is this: God leveled the house of the wicked, removing its roof (head), laying it bare to its very foundation (should "neck" in the literal translation be understood as "rock"?). As the house was crushed, so also was the wicked's leader (be he the ancient Egyptian Pharaoh or the Babylonian king).

Fourth, the initial line of 3:14 in the NIV reads: "With his own spear you pierced his head." The Hebrew at this point states: "You pierced with his shafts the head of his warriors." In other words, the wicked were destroyed by the very instruments with which they destroyed others. This is highly reminiscent of the theme that dominated the earlier taunt in 2:6–20: People reap what they sow. Others have interpreted this line in 3:14 to mean that the wicked, in the panic caused by the advance of God the warrior, attacked each other. Some of the ancient manuscripts change the pronoun in "his spear" to "your spear," that is, God's spear.

Fifth, the reference in the final line of verse 14 in the NIV is to "the wretched who were in hiding." The Hebrew has a different sense. It refers to the rejoicing of the wicked as they seek "to devour the meek in the secret place." This either means the wicked hide in a secret place, waiting to attack the unsuspecting meek, or they carry the meek back to a secret lair to devour them, as would a wild beast.

Sixth, Habakkuk 3:14–15 contains two historical allusions. The first of these verses reflects Jael's murder of Sisera (see Judg. 5:24–27), while the second alludes to the Exodus and God's victory at the sea.

Clearly Habakkuk's theophanic experience had profound relevance for his present situation. While he certainly reflected on the Exodus and used its imagery, he also saw the theophany as real in his own day. Notice the shift to a present emphasis in 3:14 where the wicked storm out to scatter the righteous. While the NIV reads "scatter us," the Hebrew has "scatter me." In other words, Habakkuk saw the theophany as the direct answer to his petition in 3:2 that God's mighty acts be renewed in his own day. God's promise, as depicted in the theophany, was that Habakkuk's hope would be realized. As Egypt had fallen before the warrior God in the past, so the Babylonians of the present would fall.

At the same time, the theophany has broader application; it

declares the inevitable fate of the wicked in any and every period of history. The theophany is also eschatological; it celebrates the ultimate victory that belongs to Yahweh.

C. Faith's Victory (3:16–19)

Habakkuk responds to the theophanic vision at first with great fear and agitation. The portrayal of God's awesome judgment is terrifying. Some scholars see Habakkuk's emotional state in 3:16 as an indication he is an ecstatic. But one must be careful with this kind of identification.

The word "ecstasy" often has negative connotations; in fact it comes from a Greek term that means "deranged." Habakkuk was not an ecstatic if the word means a frenzied person or one who is totally devoid of self-control. The Baal prophets in 1 Kings 18:25–29 were ecstatic in that sense. However, if the word refers to a person at a higher realm of awareness and sensitivity than normal, then Habakkuk qualifies, as do all the prophetic visionaries of the Old Testament.

Habakkuk's fear began to give way to confident trust in the middle of 3:16. What we have from this point through 3:19 is one of the Bible's truly noble statements of unconquerable faith. The prophet declares his determination to "wait patiently" for the judgment against Babylon. No matter how long it took, the judgment would eventually come; it would be in God's own time. Habakkuk was now certain that God, the righteous judge, was on His heavenly throne, in control of His world. Thus the prophet could look beyond the present struggles to the ultimate outcome and in that find invigorating hope.

How far Habakkuk had come! It was no longer the impatient "how long?" (1:2); rather it was "I will wait patiently" (3:16). Habakkuk now saw the injustices and tragic contradictions of life from a different perspective. His view had changed dramatically because of his honest doubt and searching questions and because of God's gracious responses.

Facing now the impending Babylonian invasion, Habakkuk recognizes the possibility that the situation would worsen before it got better. Not only would his people have to face the onslaught of Babylon, but they also would probably face starvation. The list of agricultural products in 3:17 is exhaustive; once these items were gone, nothing would be left to eat.

Some commentators contend that 3:17 introduces us to a situation different from that which has gone before, that is, to a natural disaster rather than to war. Consequently they suggest that 3:17–19 is a later addition to the book.

But that conclusion is not necessarily correct. In the ancient world, advancing armies lived off the land; they also destroyed the crops and livestock of the people they conquered. The prophet here envisions land stripped by an invading army rather than devastation produced by drought or some other natural calamity.

Habakkuk confidently confesses that, even if the Babylonian destruction left nothing to eat, he would "rejoice in the Lord" (3:18). For the wicked, joy exists only on life's surface— in the crops, livestock, and other material possessions; such joy lacks substance. But for the true believer genuine joy is found in God, not in what He gives; it is experienced at the depth of one's being. Though outer circumstances may be adverse, true joy thrives and expresses real life. Through it all Habakkuk declares he would "be joyful in God" (3:18).

Further, the prophet claims God as his "Savior" (3:18). Salvation here is probably meant in the sense of divine presence in the midst of present crisis as well as God's future deliverance of His people. God the Savior is Habakkuk's "strength" for living (3:19). He is more than the source of strength; He is the strength itself. In other words, God is Habakkuk's all.

As a result God makes the prophet's "feet like the feet of a deer" (3:19). The deer or gazelle is sure-footed, fleet, and able to move quickly in the face of danger. This image aptly illustrates the vitality, vigor, and strength Habakkuk received for life's difficulties. Because of such divine strength, he is enabled "to go on the heights," which symbolizes the prophet's ultimate triumph and victory of faith.[2]

---

[2] The Book of Habakkuk closes with a subscription containing an instruction to "the director of music," probably of the temple choir (3:19). The prayer of chapter 3 is to be accompanied by "stringed instruments" rather than percussion or wind. Some scholars think that strings suggest a triumphant mood, which would certainly be appropriate for Habakkuk 3.

For Further Study on Habakkuk

1. In what ways does the Book of Habakkuk give a believer permission to question God?

2. In the light of Habakkuk's message, how can you personally apply the premise that God will sometimes let things get worse before they get better?

3. Read about the Chaldeans in a Bible dictionary. Consider their history as well as their association with Babylon.

4. What does Habakkuk 2:2–3 teach you about the nature of Old Testament prophecy?

5. Reread the discussion of Habakkuk 2:1. How do the prophet's actions in this verse personally apply to you?

6. Habakkuk 2:4 is quoted in three New Testament passages: Romans 1:17, Galatians 3:11, and Hebrews 10:38. Examine the quotation in each setting. What are the differences and similarities in the four passages?

7. The writer of Hebrews 10:37 quotes Habakkuk 2:3, applying it to the Second Coming of Christ. What light does this quotation shed on the way the New Testament writers used the Old Testament?

8. What purpose(s) do you see for the section of "woes" in Habakkuk 2:6–20? Of what help is this section for us today?

9. Reread Habakkuk 2:18–19. Since we do not worship idols of wood and stone today, how does a passage like this apply to us?

10. Reread Habakkuk 3. How would you explain the visionary experiences of the Old Testament prophets to someone?

Chapter 7

An Introduction to Zephaniah and His Prophecy

The last three decades of the seventh century B.C. were momentous for Judah. At the outset of this period, the Assyrians' oppressive tyranny was coming to an end. Consequently Judah enjoyed a brief period of freedom from foreign intervention. Decisions the nation would make during this time would have long-term consequences.

Onto this stage in history stepped the young prophet Zephaniah. With the themes of the great eighth-century prophets serving as his solid foundation, he applied God's Word to the moment at hand. The bulk of his short message describes God's approaching judgment, primarily on Judah, yet also on all the world. But judgment was by no means the last word for Zephaniah. In the divine purpose, judgment was designed to purify, to purge, and ultimately to produce a new order.

The key to Zephaniah's proclamation is seen in the striking contrast of his first sermon with his last. Following the title in Zephaniah 1:1, the prophet cites Yahweh's frightening declaration: "I will sweep away everything from the face of the earth." Yet the message does not end there. In stark contrast is Yahweh's concluding statement to chastened, humbled Judah: "I will give you honor and praise among all the peoples of the earth when I restore your fortunes before your very eyes" (3:20). Through divine judgment Judah would come to salvation and blessing!

A. Zephaniah the Man

Information about Zephaniah is sparse, coming primarily from the book that bears his name. In fact, he is mentioned only in the book's first verse. Information about him from the remaining verses is drawn by inference only. Zephaniah is mentioned nowhere else in the Bible. Some extracanonical materials purportedly written by Zephaniah have no historical value.

Many items of interest are missing from Zephaniah's biographical sketch. We are not told of his birthplace; the experience of his call; or the date, occasion, and circumstances of his death. As is often the case in the Old Testament, the prophet fades into the background of his book, the better to emphasize God's message.

1. Zephaniah's Name

Hebrew names were often formed by combining two words. Such is true in Zephaniah's case. One part of the prophet's name is the divine name "Yahweh." This special covenant name for God appears in Hebrew in the letters that are transliterated "iah" in our English versions. The second word involved in Zephaniah's name is the Hebrew verb *ṣāphan,* which means "to hide" or "to treasure."

In light of this evidence, commentators offer several possible translations for the name "Zephaniah." These include: "he whom Yahweh has hidden," "Yahweh has guarded," "Yahweh has treasured," "Yahweh protects," "Yahweh shelters," "Yahweh conceals," and "Yahweh is protector."

We learned earlier that Old Testament names often reveal significant factors about the bearer. In the case of Zephaniah, the name may reflect God's gracious protection for one either born or called to his prophetic ministry during the days of the cruel Manasseh. This king "shed so much innocent blood that he filled Jerusalem from end to end" (2 Kings 21:16); thus the prophet's name may indicate that God "hid" or "protected" him until the time was right for his public ministry to begin. The prophet's genealogy makes it likely that he was indeed born during Manasseh's reign.

2. Zephaniah's Family

No prophet's genealogical record compares to that of Zephaniah (see 1:1). Eight of the prophets do not even mention their family tree; six of them identify only their father. Zechariah mentions both his father and grandfather. Only Zephaniah traces his heritage back four generations to his great-great-grandfather.

Most commentators feel the reason for this expanded genealogical record is the citation of Hezekiah as the final name in the list. Was this Hezekiah the Judean king?

Those scholars who are unwilling to equate the two contend that if Zephaniah had indeed meant to tell us that he was descended from royalty, he would have designated Hezekiah as the king. Some argue that Judean kings are never mentioned for the first time in Old Testament books without the title being given.

These arguments seem weak. Certainly King Hezekiah was so famous his identity must have been assumed often without any mention of title. Several commentators note that the royal designation for Hezekiah in Zephaniah 1:1 would have produced a somewhat awkward reading in Hebrew since Josiah is identified as "king of Judah" in the same verse. Furthermore, it is necessary to remember that linear genealogies were written to affirm the prophet's position and authority. The last name in the list was the most important. Thus it would seem strange for Zephaniah to trace his heritage back to Hezekiah if the latter were not indeed Judah's ancient king. No earlier Hezekiah of any great fame is known in the Old Testament.

Yet another argument against identifying the Hezekiah of Zephaniah 1:1 as the king is that three generations (Amariah, Gedaliah, Cushi) are given between Hezekiah and Zephaniah, whereas only two (Manasseh, Amon) occur between Hezekiah and Josiah, in whose reign Zephaniah preached. This argument is also weak. Early marriages in Judah could easily account for the three generations between Hezekiah and Zephaniah. At the same time, Manasseh's long life and reign explain the shorter genealogical record of the royal dynasty from Hezekiah to Josiah (see 2 Kings 21:1).

While the position certainly cannot be defended dogmatically, it seems most reasonable to conclude that Zephaniah listed Hezekiah to note his own connection with the royal family. At the very least, the genealogy indicates that the prophet was from an illustrious and distinguished family.

In addition to Hezekiah, Zephaniah's family tree also mentions his father Cushi, his grandfather Gedaliah (whose name means "Yahweh is great"), and his great-grandfather Amariah (whose name means "Yahweh promises"). The use of the divine name Yahweh in all of these names, with the exception of Cushi, is perhaps another indication of the royal blood in Zephaniah's family. Judah's kings often used the divine name in their own.

So Zephaniah the prophet was probably, though not conclusively, the great-great-grandson of King Hezekiah. As such, he was himself a man of royal blood, a cousin of King Josiah, in whose reign he ministered. His book reveals his familiarity with Judah's royal court and his condemnation of its excesses.

3. Zephaniah's Home

Although Zephaniah's birthplace is not revealed in this book, evidence points to Jerusalem as the site of his preaching. Association of the prophet with the Judean capital is based on several factors, chief of which is his comment in Zephaniah 1:4. In a discussion of God's judgment against Jerusalem the prophet refers to "this place," indicating that he is actually in the city.

Other factors associating Zephaniah with Jerusalem include his references to specific locations within Jerusalem (1:10–11), his familiarity with the various classes of people who live there (1:4, 8, 11; 3:3–4), and his eyewitness description of certain practices carried on by Jerusalem's citizens (1:5–6, 8–9, 11–12; 3:1–2).

4. Zephaniah's Date

We are told in Zephaniah 1:1 that the prophet's ministry took place during King Josiah's reign (640–609 B.C.). Though some scholars question the historical accuracy of this title, the majority seem willing to accept it. To place Zephaniah in Josiah's reign, however, is only the initial consideration. Can it

be determined more precisely when in this reign he prophe-
sied?

Josiah initiated a major religious reformation, around which
his long reign can be rather roughly divided into three parts:
(1) the pre-reformation period from 640 to 628 B.C.; (2) the
reformation itself from 628 to 622 B.C.; and (3) the post-reformation period from 622 to 609 B.C. The climactic year of the reform
came in 622 B.C. when the Book of the Law (believed now by
most to have been a major part of Deuteronomy) was found in
the temple.

Most commentators believe the conditions described in
Zephaniah's book fit best the period prior to Josiah's reform.
However, the early years of the reformation (before Josiah had
accomplished all he set out to do) may also be reflected.
Accordingly, Zephaniah may have preached in the period from
630 to 625 B.C. If so, his ministry would be contemporary with
Jeremiah's early ministry and also with the labors of Nahum.

Zephaniah's preaching denounces: syncretistic religious
practice, the worship of astral deities, Judah's adoption of
foreign dress and religious customs, in addition to skepticism
and indifference toward Yahweh (1:4–5, 8–9, 12). These were
the kinds of evils attacked by the Josianic reform (see 2 Kings
23:4–5, 12).

Those who feel the prophecy was written in the post-
reformation period of Josiah's reign appeal primarily to two
arguments.[1] First, they call attention to God's threat to "punish
the princes and the king's sons" (1:8). Since Josiah was only
eight years old when he became king and twenty when he
started the reformation, advocates of the later dating contend

---

[1] One problem passage debated by the various sides in this discussion is
Zephaniah 1:4, where God declares that He will cut off from Jerusalem "every
remnant of Baal." Some scholars see this as a clear indication that Zephaniah
preached after the reform had been inaugurated (628 B.C.), but before it had been
completed (622 B.C.). In other words, when Zephaniah preached, the Josianic
reform had eradicated some, but not all, of the Baal worship. God would now
remove the rest. However, one simple explanation for the passage is that God
intends to destroy all Baal worship—even down to the last remnant. If this
explanation is true, the passage could easily date from the period before 628 B.C.
Furthermore, the LXX presents an alternate reading that, if correct, completely
removes the passage from the debate over Zephaniah's date. The LXX translates
"every remnant of Baal" as "the names of Baal."

that his sons were much too young in the pre-reformation period to be accountable for sinful acts.[2] This argument is easily answered when we recognize that the phrases "king's sons" and "princes" need not refer to Josiah's sons. They may refer to sons or even grandsons of the earlier kings, Manasseh and Amon.

Those who would date Zephaniah's ministry in the post-reformation period of Josiah's reign also argue that the prophet was strongly influenced by the Book of Deuteronomy.[3] Since the Book of the Law was not discovered in the temple until 622 B.C., these scholars contend that Zephaniah must have written later. This view implies that no Deuteronomic influence could be felt until after the lawbook's discovery. No doubt that discovery was of great significance. But does that mean that the Deuteronomic ideas first appeared on the scene that year? When was that particular copy of the ancient law written? Who had had access to it earlier? Were there other copies? Could not prophetic schools in Jerusalem have had contact with its ideas for years? It seems unwise to declare dogmatically that Zephaniah was not exposed to Deuteronomic thought until after 622 B.C. We have too little insight into the history of the text's transmission to make final statements on such matters.

Another factor to consider when attempting to date Zephaniah's ministry is the international scene reflected by his book. The backdrop to his proclamation includes military movements, invasions, and political upheaval (see 1:14–18; 2:4–15; 3:6). Does this kind of turmoil fit the scene of 630–625 B.C., the date suggested above for his ministry?

Older commentaries generally point to the large-scale military movements of the Scythians in the period around 630 B.C. These fierce, ruthless people from southern Russia supposedly, at one time or another, fought Assyrians, Syrians, Phoenicians, and Egyptians, among others. But no evidence indicates they ever fought Judah. Many scholars suggest they are the unnamed military power behind Zephaniah 1 and Jeremiah

---

[2]When Josiah inaugurated the reform in 628 B.C., his son Jehoiakim was six, Jehoahaz was four, and Zedekiah had not yet been born.

[3]To compare the two books, consider the following: (1) Zephaniah 1:13 and Deuteronomy 28:30, 39; (2) Zephaniah 1:16–17 and Deuteronomy 28:28–29, 52; and (3) Zephaniah 3:5 and Deuteronomy 32:4.

4–6. Unfortunately our only source for the Scythian invasions is the ancient historian Herodotus, whose works were often colored by legend. Today many have abandoned the Scythian hypothesis completely. Others recognize that we know very little about the Scythians' role in the violent political upheavals in the last half of the seventh century B.C. It now seems unlikely they were the "occasion" for Zephaniah's preaching.

But the Scythians were certainly not the only cause of turmoil in the period from 630 to 625 B.C. This was a catastrophic time for Assyria, which for a century had been the ancient world's dominant power. Though the exact course of events is not known, it is evident that the Assyrian kingdom was beginning to come apart at the seams. Asshurbanapal, the last great king, died about 627 B.C. Even then the Medes were ready to attack Assyria. The Babylonians did in fact defeat the Assyrians in a major battle late in 626 B.C. Surely the volatile scene caused by the breakdown of Assyrian power and the emergence of the Babylonian state could have, to some degree, occasioned Zephaniah's preaching.

But in discussing the influence of the international scene on Zephaniah, we must stress one other point—we do not have to match all of Zephaniah's political projections with history as we know it. As already indicated, it is next to impossible to relate the Scythian invasion with all of the events in Zephaniah 2:4–15. Likewise the prophet's political forecasts do not all fit the downfall of Assyria and the rise of Babylon. We must recognize that Zephaniah, while to some degree reflecting history, was also speaking the language of eschatology, foretelling the future that God would bring to pass. For Zephaniah it was God Himself who was bringing judgment against the nations. The prophet was not so much concerned with the *agents* of the coming judgment as he was with its *certainty*. Whether the Scythian invasion or the emergence of Babylon, these events merely provided a background for the prophet's portrayal of the day of Yahweh's wrath. To narrow Zephaniah's political forecasts to one specific historical event is to miss the point.

Having now placed Zephaniah's ministry in the period around 630 to 625 B.C., we must consider briefly other significant dates in the prophet's experience. If the earlier identification of Hezekiah in Zephaniah 1:1 with the Judean king is indeed correct, Zephaniah's birth would have come sometime in the reign of King Manasseh (687–642 B.C.). To pinpoint the year precisely is impossible, though the period demanded by the length of years in the genealogy would seem to compress the date to the last of Manasseh's reign. It seems safe to suggest 650 B.C. as a possible date for the prophet's birth.

The date of Zephaniah's call also is not given. However, if we accept 650 B.C. as the date of his birth and 630 B.C. as the beginning of his ministry, the obvious conclusion is that he was a youth when he was called. It is significant to remember the youthfulness of Zephaniah's contemporaries, Jeremiah (see Jer. 1:6) and Josiah (who was twenty when the reformation began). One can well imagine the youthful zeal of these three in their efforts to bring change to Judah in the 630 to 620 B.C. decade.

We know neither the length of Zephaniah's ministry nor the date of his death. Perhaps the brevity of his prophecy suggests a ministry of short duration.

Thus we see that Zephaniah was born about 650 B.C. He was a youth when God called him to his prophetic role, and his ministry started in the years just prior to Josiah's reformation. He never mentioned the reform, which may indicate that his ministry ended before the reform began, though it is possible he preached for a brief time after its inception. It is not too far afield to suggest that the young prophet of royal blood may have been one of the major influences on Josiah as the young king envisioned and inaugurated his major reformation.

5. Zephaniah's Occupation

Nowhere in the Book of Zephaniah is the prophet's occupation revealed. Some commentators, however, feel he was either a professional prophet in the Jerusalem temple or a priest on the temple staff. Clues for this view are found scattered throughout the book: Zephaniah 1:7 (the background of which was perhaps a sacrifice on a festival day), 2:1 (the prophet calls the people to a solemn assembly), and 3:10 (the prophet leads Israel in a worship celebration).

But do such passages really place Zephaniah on the temple

staff? For years in Old Testament studies an extreme view contended that the prophets were radically separated from Israel's official worship, even to the point that they wanted to do away with the sacrificial system. Today scholarship recognizes (as the biblical evidence seems to show) that a working relationship existed between some of the prophets and the worship at the temple. Jeremiah, for example, had a priestly background (see Jer. 1:1), while Habakkuk, as we saw earlier, may have been associated with the religious establishment. At the same time, to recognize this relationship is not necessarily to say that the prophets were on the temple staff. Nor does it say that they did not receive Yahweh's Word and proclaim it at His command, sometimes even in opposition to what was done in the official worship (see Isa. 1:10–15; Jer. 7:1–15).

Therefore while the view that Zephaniah was on the temple staff cannot be totally dismissed, neither can it be verified. In fact it seems safe to suggest that any person acquainted with the rituals of Israelite worship could have used Zephaniah's language. We simply cannot draw any conclusion about his vocation. He is known to us only as one called by God from the Hebrew society to deliver the divine message at a particular moment in history.

6. Zephaniah's Personality

Whereas Zephaniah's contemporary, Jeremiah, revealed much of his personality, Zephaniah remains for the most part hidden behind his message. Yet as we examine his book, dimensions of his personality become evident.

For example, Zephaniah was a man of intense passion and moral sensitivity. He saw clearly the rebellion of Judah and other nations against God. His convictions about this were so strong he refused to compromise his condemnation of their sin. Consequently he comes across to many readers as a grim, sober, humorless person, seemingly obsessed with judgment and doom.

Yet Zephaniah was also an optimist, a joyful man who could call for song and praise (3:14). Though some scholars deny that he wrote the passages of hope in the book, no good reason exists to do so. Zephaniah preached judgment, but he also believed

.t God would bring forth from the devastation a new era of
eace.

In addition, Zephaniah was a man of profound spirituality.
He believed that one's relationship with God was to be taken
with utmost seriousness; he lamented the indifference and
external worship that reflected a person devoid of inward
spiritual reality (1:12).

Zephaniah was also a man of great boldness and courage.
His messages of judgment were delivered against those who
were in a position to do him harm (1:8; 3:3–4). Yet he never
strayed from straightforward, unflinching proclamations of judgment.

Finally, Zephaniah was a youthful aristocrat. Coming from
the royal family, he focused his attention more on the ruling
classes than on the common person. While he was aware of the
plight of society's downtrodden, he did not make their situation
a major emphasis of his preaching as did his predecessors, Amos
and Micah. Again we are reminded that God uses different kinds
of people for various types of ministry.

B. Zephaniah the Book

The Book of Zephaniah is the ninth in the collection of
twelve Old Testament minor prophets. Its Hebrew text is of
good quality, though the LXX offers helpful variant readings for
a few isolated passages.

1. The Nature of the Literature in Zephaniah

The Book of Zephaniah is poetry, though most scholars
contend it does not rank as high as that of other prophets like
Nahum, Isaiah, and Jeremiah. This judgment is not necessarily
correct. One of the most enduring Christian hymns is based on
Zephaniah's dramatic picture of the day of Yahweh.[4]

Certainly Zephaniah's language is clear and forceful, imagi-
native and emotional; he has no difficulty communicating the

---

[4]The medieval hymn is entitled "Dies Irae, Dies Illa." It was written by
Thomas of Celano (1190–1260 A.D.), a companion of Francis of Assisi, and has
been translated into many modern languages. The Latin introductory words
reflect the Vulgate translation of Zephaniah's passage; Thomas applied the
passage to the Last Judgment.

urgency of his message. No other prophet more forcefully describes judgment than this kinsman of royalty.

Determination of poetic meter in Zephaniah is subject to debate. Most commentators who treat this issue recognize several rhythmical schemes in the book, with the Qinah or dirge measure being the most prevalent.[5] It is not surprising to find varying metrical patterns. The prophets exercised great freedom in their use of literary forms. They were not, after all, poets in the first place, but rather God's proclaimers who used poetic forms to express divine truth.

The Book of Zephaniah is also prophetic literature. Its location in the canon verifies this conclusion. Traditional forms of prophetic proclamation also fill the book. These include: the lament (1:10–11); the exhortation (2:1–3); oracles against foreign nations (2:4–15); the prophetic woe or invective threat (3:1–8); and oracles of promise (3:9–20). The oracles against foreign nations contain taunt-songs, yet another prophetic literary device.

Some commentators think that Zephaniah's prophecy contains elements of apocalyptic writing. Certainly the eschatological emphasis that seems on occasion to be removed from history itself borders on apocalyptic. However, other features of this type of writing (for example, angelology, demonology, numerology, a messiah) are missing. It is best to conclude that no strong case for the apocalyptic character of Zephaniah can be constructed.

2. Critical Problems in the Book of Zephaniah

Is Zephaniah the human author of the book that bears his name? If so, how much of the material can actually be ascribed to him? These are issues that have troubled scholarship ever since J. G. Eichhorn concluded in 1824 that Zephaniah 2:13–15 was not written by Zephaniah. Today scholars have judged virtually every part of the book to be alien to Zephaniah's thought.

While most scholars consider chapter 1 (with the exception

---

[5] Examples of this meter in Zephaniah occur in the Hebrew readings of the following passages: 1:17; 2:4, 6–9, and 13–15. Unfortunately the English translation loses the effect.

of the title) to be primarily from Zephaniah, they also conclude that a great amount of editorial revision has occurred in the chapter. Chapters 2 and 3 do not fare as well. Many believe the bulk of this material was written by someone other than Zephaniah. The most universal evaluation of "non-genuine" material is reserved for the book's last section, the great passage of hope in Zephaniah 3:14–20.

Reasons for these conclusions are many and complicated. Some commentators fill a dozen pages with discussions of the book's integrity and the possible revisions at different stages of Israelite history. For the sake of convenience, let us consider three areas of concern that have led some to attribute sections of the book to authors and editors other than Zephaniah.

First, some commentators simply cannot accept the idea that prophets of doom could also be prophets of hope. Accordingly they assert that later editors suppressed the original judgmental and negative conclusions of books like Amos and Zephaniah by appending to them oracles of salvation. Such comforting messages supposedly reflect post-exilic circumstances, when the disaster of the Exile was past and that tragedy was to be transformed into triumph.

Second, some of the phraseology and the circle of ideas in Zephaniah, especially in the last two chapters, are said to be from the exilic or post-exilic periods rather than from the age of Zephaniah. Cited at this point are such concepts as the following: (1) the "humble of the land" (2:3); (2) "the remnant of the house of Judah" (2:7) and "the remnant of Israel" (3:13); (3) "the law" (3:4); (4) the conversion of all peoples (3:9); and (5) the gathering of the Diaspora (3:10).

Third, some argue that the historical allusions in chapter 2 do not fit the time of the pre-Josianic reform. An example often noted is the animosity of Moab and Ammon toward Judah in Zephaniah 2:8. Opponents of Zephaniah's authorship contend this animosity is from the period of Jerusalem's fall (around 587 B.C.) and not from Zephaniah's day. They cite Ezekiel 25:1–11 as their proof text.

Quite frankly, all of these arguments are arbitrary and subjective. They are often based on insufficient evidence. Commentators who question Zephaniah's authorship even differ greatly among themselves as to which passages should be considered "genuine" (primary) and which "non-genuine" (secondary). Consequently their arguments simply are not convincing.

On the other hand, consider the other side of the above-mentioned objections to Zephaniah's authorship. First, why could not a prophet of judgment offer a message of hope? Does not the larger context of biblical theology anticipate such a message? Is not God by grace working to bring about a new order? Why could not a prophet who predicted the fall of his people have hope for and divine insight into a new day? The eschatological kingdom of God is ever apparent in Scripture.

Second, some of the ideas mentioned in Zephaniah may have been significant in the exilic or post-exilic periods. But does that automatically negate the possibility of their significance in another time?

Consider, for example, the concept of the remnant, which critics of Zephaniah's authorship contend was developed after the exilic experience. But was not the remnant a major teaching in Isaiah's theology one century before Zephaniah's day? Of course one could say that the concept was added to Isaiah's book just as it was added to Zephaniah's. But does that then mean that the later editor even changed the theologically significant name of Isaiah's son Shear-Jashub ("a remnant will return") in Isaiah 7? All of the ideas mentioned above as post-exilic have a place in pre-exilic thought.

Third, several issues could be raised about historical matters like the Ammonite-Moabite animosity toward Judah. Could it not be admitted, for example, that our historical information throughout the Old Testament period is to some degree spotty? While there was obviously the conflict at the time of Jerusalem's fall, could there not have also been other times of conflict for which we have no record?

Also if our earlier discussion of Zephaniah's birth date is accurate, he could still have been alive around 587 B.C. Could he not have written much of the book early in his ministry and added some later? Furthermore, the fact that Zephaniah *predicted* a general and universal judgment negates the need to match each foreign oracle with some known event. The prophet was underscoring the reality of future judgment, not the agent or the specific details.

Scholars argue that the literary analysis of biblical materials and the alignment of sections with certain stages of history help us better understand the Scripture as well as understand that it was—and is—a living message. I could not agree more! But while it is important to try to see the growth and transmission of the text where we can, we must also admit that what we have is the final canonical copy; anytime we try to go behind it to piece together its compilation history, we are on subjective ground. When commentators differ so widely in their conclusions, it would seem safe to exercise caution in going against the accepted canonical tradition. In that light, while it may be that editorial additions have occurred in Zephaniah (the title perhaps), no valid reason exists to deny any of the book to the prophet.

To accept Zephaniah as the author of the book does not mean that he sat down and wrote it from cover to cover. More than likely, what we have is a collection of sermons and sermon summaries from different periods in the prophet's life, joined together not so much by chronology as by purpose. The book is a literary unit that develops in logical sequence the major themes of judgment, purification, and restoration. The themes are incomplete without each other.

3. Influences on the Writing of Zephaniah

The great prophets of the eighth century B.C.—Amos, Hosea, Isaiah, and Micah—are especially significant in the Old Testament story. It is not surprising that the writings of each made major contributions to Zephaniah's thought nearly a century later. Some contemporary authors have even gone so far as to suggest that Zephaniah depended on his predecessors to such a degree that he demonstrated no creativity in thought or literary expression.

While this judgment is too harsh, it is true that Zephaniah relied heavily on the earlier writings. He frequently reshaped them to address the turbulent last years of the seventh century B.C. We could even conclude that one of his chief contributions was the application of the eighth-century B.C. prophets' theology to his own day.

The influence of Amos on Zephaniah is seen primarily in the development of the "day of Yahweh" concept (Amos 5:18–20; Zeph. 1:14–2:3). Hosea contributed an emphasis on the suffering of nature because of sin (Hos. 4:1–3; Zeph. 1:2–3). Micah influenced Zephaniah's understanding of the remnant community (Mic. 5:7–8; Zeph. 2:7; 3:11–13).

But it was Isaiah who really contributed to Zephaniah's preaching. This is not strange when one considers the ancient tradition that Isaiah too was of Judah's royal family. Through his writings, the royal prophet of the eighth century uniquely became the mentor of the royal prophet of the seventh century B.C. The survey of Zephaniah's theology in the following section illustrates Isaiah's profound influence on Zephaniah.[6]

4. Major Theological Themes in the Book of Zephaniah

Zephaniah was not a systematic theologian. He was first and foremost a preacher. Any effort, therefore, to systematize his theology runs the risk of misrepresenting his thought. It cannot be overemphasized that each theological concept must first be seen in the context of the prophetic proclamation. However, if a commentator has done that basic work, it is valuable to present a survey of the theology as introductory information. It is with that background that the major themes of Zephaniah's theology are offered here in systematic fashion.

First, for Zephaniah, the major sin of humanity is pride (Zeph. 2:10; 3:11). Pride leads to rebellion against God and His authority (Zeph. 3:1–4). It manifests itself in insolence (Zeph. 2:15; 3:1–2, 4), idolatry (Zeph. 1:4–6, 8–9), and injustice (Zeph. 1:7–13; 3:3–5). It leads to a complacent, indifferent, self-satisfied, skeptical, cynical lifestyle that in turn creates a lack of concern for life's genuine priorities (Zeph. 1:6, 12). And for Zephaniah, people were morally responsible to God for such sin. Isaiah had earlier emphasized the same ideas (Isa. 5:18–21; 9:9; 16:6; 23:9; 25:11).

Second, for Zephaniah, God's response to sin is judgment,

---

[6] For additional examples of Isaiah's influence on Zephaniah compare Zephaniah 1:7 to Isaiah 34:6 and Zephaniah 2:14 to Isaiah 13:21 and 34:11. Other passages that serve as background to Zephaniah's message include Isaiah 30:19–33; 31:8–9; and 32:16–18.

which is to be manifested through the "day of Yahweh" (Zeph. 1:7–10; 1:14–2:3). The prophet saw that great day as imminent (Zeph. 1:14), terrible (Zeph. 1:15–17), and universal (Zeph. 3:8). It would devastate Judah (Zeph. 1:4–2:3), the various nations of the world (Zeph. 2:4–15), and nature itself (Zeph. 1:2–3). Nothing could halt the action of God's wrath (Zeph. 1:18). No longer was God waiting for the slow progress of ethical reform; rather now with one sweep of His mighty arm evil would be judged and removed (Zeph. 1:17–18). Once again Isaiah's influence on Zephaniah is easily seen (Isa. 2:6–22).

Third, for Zephaniah, God's judgment has a positive dimension that was to be demonstrated through the purified remnant community (Zeph. 2:7; 3:9–20). In other words, Zephaniah, like his predecessor Isaiah, believed the great day of judgment was designed for corrective as well as punitive purposes (Isa. 1:24–31; 4:2–6; 6:13; 7:3; 10:20–23; 28:5). Judgment would lead to pure worship whereby nations would serve Yahweh with one accord (Zeph. 3:9–10). Israel would return to its land humbled and purified (Zeph. 3:10–13). This remnant community would consist of the meek and the humble, those who responded to the call for repentance and genuinely trusted in Yahweh. They would experience the restoration of their fortunes and praise among the people (Zeph. 3:14–20). Happiness would be undisturbed because Yahweh their king would be with His people.

This final theme reveals Zephaniah's theological starting place. Basic to the prophet's proclamation is that God is at work in this fallen world. His eternal purposes will be fulfilled despite humanity's sinfulness. Out of the chaotic corruption caused by sin, God will create a new order.

When one recognizes Zephaniah's theological center, it is an easy matter to see why the passages of hope conclude the book. Those who contend that the last verses are from a different author and another time fail to recognize Zephaniah's understanding of God, His nature, and His work in the world.

Chapter 8

The Dark Day of Judgment
(Zephaniah 1:1–3:8)

Called to preach in a day of unspeakable worldliness and callous indifference to spiritual realities, Zephaniah proclaimed a message that is very bleak. It is a message of universal judgment and terror. It is an announcement of the coming great day of Yahweh's wrath on Judah and the world's nations.

Though the book for the most part is negative, even terrifying, its final note is positive. God will bring Judah and the nations through the judgment, purifying them, thereby creating a new order.

This chapter of our study will examine the negative aspect of Zephaniah's message. The three major divisions are: (A) The Title of the Book (1:1); (B) The Prediction of Universal Judgment (1:2–3); and (C) The Judgment Against Nations (1:4–3:8).

A. The Title of the Book (1:1)

The Book of Zephaniah opens with the same kind of introductory formula found in several other Old Testament prophecies (see Hos. 1:1; Joel 1:1; Mic. 1:1) though, as mentioned earlier, the genealogical record is unusually long. This introduction gives information about the prophecy's author, his family, and the date of his prophetic activity.

The most significant factor in the title is found in the initial statement: "The word of the LORD that came to Zephaniah." *How* Zephaniah perceived the Word we are not told; *that* he perceived it *as God's Word* is certain.

The prophet's own role in the matter should not be negated. Though he was to be God's messenger, he was not a programmed robot. In fact it was through Zephaniah's own living experience with God that the message was formed and shaped. The Hebrew word translated "came" is perhaps better understood in this context by translations like "happened" or "experienced." The Word "happened" to Zephaniah; he "experienced" the Word as the living reality of God's presence.

The title thus verifies that the Book of Zephaniah is a product of divine revelation through human instrumentality. It is both Word of God and word of man. The human factor in the prophetic word in no way denies the book's authority, which is derived from God alone.

B. The Prediction of Universal Judgment (1:2–3)

It is doubtful a more negative introduction has ever been given to a sermon than the one Zephaniah offers. In words reminiscent of the flood story in Genesis (see Gen. 6:7; 7:21–23), the prophet predicts a universal judgment. Destruction will come not only to humanity, on whose shoulders responsibility rests for the tragic event, but also to the created world for which humanity was responsible (see Ps. 8:6–8).

Nature's suffering should not be interpreted as mere poetic license or literary coloring. Rather the passage is one of many in the Bible that emphasizes that human sin against God negatively affects creation itself. In other words, the entire earth experiences the consequences of human rebellion. Classic statements of this idea are found in Genesis 3:17 and Romans 8:22. While much biblical evidence points to the ultimate redemption of nature,[1] Zephaniah here focuses only on the negative.

One part of verse 3 is difficult. The NIV renders the disputed passage: "The wicked will have only heaps of rubble." A literal translation of the Hebrew text reads: "and the stumbling blocks with the wicked." The stumbling blocks evidently represent those things that lead people to reject God (idols, for example, or other enticements to sin). In this light, the passage

---

[1] Nature's redemption is seen in passages like Isaiah 11:6–9; Colossians 1:20; and Revelation 22:1–3.

reveals that God will sweep away everything—people, animals, birds, fish, "and the stumbling blocks with the wicked."

This passage is terrifying in its universal scope and uncompromising severity. Yahweh is revealed as the consuming God. But the emphasis should not strike us as strange. God is a righteous deity. Consequently judgment against sin is a certainty. Though the message of judgment is difficult to deliver, the prophetic voice must declare it. Zephaniah was on the historical scene for just such a time.

C. The Judgment Against Nations (1:4–3:8)

Having predicted universal judgment, Zephaniah moves from the general to the specific. This section, which comprises the bulk of his message, relates the judgment to individual nations. The lengthy passage can be outlined as follows: (1) The Judgment of Judah and Jerusalem (1:4–2:3); (2) The Judgment of Judah's Neighbors (2:4–15); and (3) A Reiteration of Judgment on Jerusalem and the Nations (3:1–8).

1. The Judgment of Judah and Jerusalem (1:4–2:3)

Zephaniah's main focus is on the fate of his own nation. God had called Judah into a special relationship, but that relationship had been severed. Judah now faced God's wrath.

The following outline helps clarify this part of Zephaniah's sermon: (a) The Cause of Judgment (1:4–6); (b) The Extent of Judgment (1:7–13); (c) The Terror of Judgment (1:14–18); and (d) The Shelter from Judgment (2:1–3).

a. The Cause of Judgment (1:4–6). Blatant worship of false deities, syncretistic worship practices, outright apostasy, and religious indifference characterized the Judah of Zephaniah's day. In Jerusalem it was very difficult to distinguish true worship from false. People both with divided theological allegiance and with no theological allegiance populated the city. Considered by earlier prophets to be the prospective religious capital of the world (see Isa. 2:2–4; Mic. 4:1–3), the Jerusalem of Zephaniah's day was instead the center of idolatry and apostasy. The city's inhabitants were idolatrous down to the last person (notice "all who live in Jerusalem" in verse 4).[2]

It was this religious corruption that had severed the covenant relationship with God and was now the cause of His judgment against both nation and city. God's mighty, out-stretched hand in happier days had led Israel out of bondage (see Deut. 26:8), but now it would deliver a devastating blow (1:4ab).

Following the terse warning of impending divine action, Zephaniah describes the various aspects of idolatry that were prevalent in his land. His list of items is probably representative rather than exhaustive.

He first considers the objects of idolatry and their coming destruction: "I will cut off from this place every remnant of Baal" (1:4c). Baal was the most popular deity of Canaanite religion; he was a fertility god whose worship involved "sacred" prostitution. The temptation to follow Baal had long plagued Israel and was a major emphasis in the preaching of prophets like Elijah, Hosea, and Jeremiah. While Zephaniah may be referring to the worship of the old Canaanite Baal, his statement might also represent idolatry in all its forms. Whatever the specific emphasis, be it Baal worship in a narrow or broad sense, every vestige of it would be obliterated by God's judgment.

Zephaniah next considers the priests of idolatry (1:4d). The Hebrew text at this point specifically mentions two clas-sifications of priests. The passage literally reads: "the name of the idol-priests with the priests." The first term (kemarim) refers to those who actually serve gods other than Yahweh, whereas the second (kohanim) is used for priests of the true God who encourage idolatrous practice either by their indifference to its existence or by the inconsistency of their lives. The prophet envisions total destruction for both groups; their very names will be lost to memory.

Finally Zephaniah considers various classes of idol wor-shipers (1:5-6). He first mentions those involved in the outright

---

[2] Perhaps the "all" is poetic exaggeration, for Zephaniah suggests the possibility of a responsible remnant in chapters 2:1-3 and 3:11-13.

worship of false gods, exemplified by those who worship "the starry host" (1:5a).[3] Worship of astral deities was broadly practiced in the biblical world. It had gained increasing influence in Judah under the Assyrian domination, particularly during the reigns of Manasseh and Amon (687–640 B.C.).

Another group of idolaters Zephaniah notes were those of divided allegiance (1:5b). They tried to worship Yahweh at the same time they worshiped other deities. They would "bow down and swear by the LORD and . . . also swear by Molech."

Some commentators debate the meaning of the word rendered "Molech" by the NIV. The Hebrew word used here literally reads "their king." Some feel it alludes either to Baal, who is referred to as a king on ancient inscriptions, or to any false deity accepted by Judah's idolaters as their king. However, many commentators identify the word as the name "Milcom," who was the god of the Ammonites. Others, like the NIV, see the word as a reference to the Phoenician god Molech, a deity whose worship involved sacrificing children.

Regardless of the god's identity, the meaning of the passage is certain. The people would swear "to" Yahweh (where the NIV reads "by" the Hebrew has "to"). That is, they would declare their homage and allegiance to Him; they also would swear "by" Molech, that is, they would bind themselves by oath and lifestyle to Molech. As the Bible often declares, allegiance to two masters is impossible (see Josh. 24:14–27; 1 Sam. 7:3; 1 Kings 18:21; Matt. 6:24).

Zephaniah mentions a third class of idolaters in verse 6a: "Those who turn back from following the LORD." These are people who for a time followed God but let other factors eventually get in the way of the relationship. They have now turned from Him. They are the apostate.

The final class Zephaniah mentions is the indifferent (1:6b). Perhaps this group is the most tragic. Their idol is self-centered-

---

[3]This worship was actually done on the housetops, which were generally flat. These idolaters would use their roofs to offer sacrifices directly to the stars rather than indirectly to images or representations of them.

ness. They see no need of God. They do not seek Him. They never ask about Him.[4] They represent the most difficult group to be reached for God. The *outright idolaters* at least see the need for deity and worship, albeit their emphasis is misplaced. Those of *divided loyalty* have some insight into their need for God, though they try to do the impossible in commitment. The *apostate* at one time followed Him. But the *religious indifferent* consider God insignificant. They have taken idolatry to its most terrifying conclusion.

In summary, the universal judgment predicted by Zephaniah was to fall especially on Judah and Jerusalem, the place of greatest responsibility. The covenant people were to have no other gods but Yahweh (Exod. 20:3). Yet this commandment had been grievously broken. Judah's idolatry was the fundamental cause of the judgment.

b. The Extent of Judgment (1:7–13). A word demanding an immediate response of reverential awe begins this section of Zephaniah's sermon. Translated by the NIV as "be silent" (1:7a), the Hebrew word *has* is similar in sound to our English word "hush," which it could also be rendered. The prophet's call for silence indicates that a solemn moment is at hand. The solemnity of the occasion is further emphasized by designating God as "the Sovereign LORD" (NIV) or "the Lord Yahweh" (literal Hebrew). The solemn occasion demanding the hush is the imminent arrival of the day of Yahweh (1:7b). According to Zephaniah, all the preparations for that great and terrible day have been completed (1:7cd).

It is not certain when or where the concept of the Day of the Lord first appeared in Israelite history. Some scholars feel it had its origins in the early days of Joshua and Judges when God often rose up on behalf of His people to defeat some foreign enemy. It seems certain that by the time of the prophets the concept had taken on a positive meaning in popular thought. The people considered the Day of the Lord to be the occasion of God's judgment against *their* enemies.

Amos, however, transformed the concept (Amos 5:18–20). It

---

[4]These Judeans had forgotten God (see Moses' warning in Deut. 6:12). All one has to do to forget Him is to do nothing at all! A vital relationship with God must be consistently nourished.

was for him a judgment day, not against Israel's enemies, but against God's enemies. For Amos these included the citizens of Israel. Isaiah several years later emphasized the same idea as he saw the day aimed against sinful Judah (Isa. 2:6–22).

Zephaniah also preaches the Day of the Lord, adopting the emphasis of Amos and Isaiah. He too saw the day directed against God's enemies but, tragically, no people of his time better fit that description than his own nation of Judah.

Using words and concepts from Hebrew worship, Zephaniah describes the imminent Day of the Lord as a sacrifice. The reverential silence for which he calls was perhaps a feature of Judah's sacrificial ritual.

In the prophet's worship illustration, it is Yahweh Himself who prepares the sacrifice (1:7c). The nature of the sacrifice becomes clear in the verses that follow—it is Judah and its citizens! Furthermore Yahweh has consecrated, that is, He has set apart or made ready the guests He has invited to the sacrifice (1:7d). Their identity is uncertain. Most commentators believe they are the armies who will destroy Judah,[5] though a few contend the Judeans themselves are the invited guests. Be that as it may, the passage's emphasis is clear—Judah is to be sacrificed because of its sin against God.

Verses 8–13 clearly reveal the terrible extent of the judgment. All classes of the population will be affected; the judgment will extend to every quarter of Jerusalem.

Zephaniah first singles out for judgment governmental figures and members of the royal court—the political leadership of the land (1:8–9). The "princes" whom Yahweh will punish are the various tribal heads, officers of the royal court, and administrative leaders.[6]

Most commentators feel "the king's sons" were various

---

[5] Some writers try to press the figures of Zephaniah's illustration too far. They worry that God prepares the sacrifice (that is, He slays it), while the guests consume it. Actually the Babylonian armies defeated Judah. We must not try to force illustrative figures too far. Regardless of the historical role the enemy armies played, the prophet sees all that happened to Judah as under God's authority and control. Thus it was God who prepared Judah as the sacrifice.

[6] The shift to the first person in verse 8 ("I will punish the princes") demonstrates Zephaniah's role as God's spokesman. Zephaniah will not punish; Yahweh will. The prophets often used the pronoun "I" when speaking for God.

brothers and uncles of King Josiah (or the royal family in general) rather than Josiah's actual children. If Zephaniah preached this message around 630 B.C., Josiah's own sons were too young to be singled out for the moral condemnation required in the verse.

Some scholars, however, suggest that the reference is to Josiah's sons because they will be Judah's rulers later when the calamity occurs. Josiah himself is not mentioned, reflecting either his own youthfulness at the time or his innocence; he was indeed a man of genuine faith (see 2 Kings 22:18–20; 2 Chron. 34:26–33).

One of the sins of the political figures was to dress "in foreign clothes." Such behavior revealed a deeper problem. Outer dress symbolized inner attitude. Those who dressed in the latest fashions from Egypt or Mesopotamia were also prone to follow the cultural influences and pagan religions of those countries. Because Zephaniah referred to "all those clad in foreign clothes," he suggests that such behavior, begun by the leadership, had ultimately been followed by those wealthy enough to afford fine fashions from foreign markets.

The first part of verse 9 ("all who avoid stepping on the threshold") has long troubled commentators. Many see it as a reference to some superstitious action or pagan religious practice, like that suggested by the story of the Philistine god Dagon in 1 Samuel 5:1–5.

Such an interpretation, however, does not seem to fit the context. Consider the phrase "the temple of their gods" (NIV) in the last part of verse 9, which is better translated "the house of their masters" (literal Hebrew). In other words, the last part of the passage has nothing whatever to do with religious action; rather it refers to the henchmen or associates of the political leaders who use "violence and deceit" to fill the coffers of those they serve. The scene is not one of religious malpractice but one of social injustice.

The troublesome first part of verse 9 becomes clear in that light. It likewise has nothing to do with pagan religious practice; it rather refers to those who are so eager to plunder their victims' homes that they "leap over the threshold" in their hurry. The expression thus stands for violent entry into another's home.

Zephaniah next focuses on God's judgment of the merchant class (1:10–11). As he foresees the imminent disaster, he describes the chaotic scene. From throughout Jerusalem come cries of terror and the noise of battle. Though some commentators see the four sites mentioned here by Zephaniah as all in the northern part of Jerusalem,[7] it is perhaps better to see them as representative of all quarters of the city. The judgment will extend to every section of Jerusalem, even as it will to every class of citizen.

Significant in verse 11 is the phrase translated "your merchants" in the NIV. The Hebrew phrase is literally translated, "the people of Canaan." In other words, by the time of Zephaniah the Judean business community had become exactly like the old pagan merchants of the earlier Canaanite settlement in the land. They were Canaanite (or pagan) in their business conduct and in their lifestyle. They did not hesitate to use dishonest practices or to live by an absorbing commitment to their secular work. Yet these were supposedly the people of the covenant! Is it any wonder that they would "be wiped out" and "ruined" on that terrible day?

The religious indifferent, which most likely made up the bulk of the population, constitute the last class of people Zephaniah singles out in this section (1:12–13). Two of the prophet's most impressive figures of speech are found in this section. In the first, Zephaniah envisions God Himself searching Jerusalem with lamps. Regardless of where sinners try to hide on the Day of the Lord, the probing, seeking, judging God will discover them. It is this passage that led medieval artists to paint Zephaniah with a lamp in his hand.

The other figure used to describe the religious indifferent is taken from the wine-making process. Zephaniah compares such people to "wine left on its dregs." Such wine has thickened and lost its flavor and strength. Similarly these citizens of Jerusalem had become self-indulgent, complacent, insensitive, indifferent

---

[7] If the four sites should all be identified one day as having been on Jerusalem's north side, it will reveal that Zephaniah was emphasizing the section of the city that would first fall to an invader. Due to topography, enemy armies found it easier to attack Jerusalem from the north. Our knowledge of the location of the four sites is tentative.

to the things of God and totally irresponsible toward the higher
priorities of life. Their self-centeredness resulted in a skeptical,
distorted theology that was incapable of perceiving God in
action. For them, God did neither good nor ill; He was totally
unconcerned about the affairs of people. If He were concerned,
He could do nothing to help or harm. These people were the
practical atheists of Judah.

Zephaniah sadly announces that these people will discover
the reality of God's action when they are devastated by His
judgment (1:13). None of their self-centered gain will aid them
when the day of judgment begins. Another way to emphasize
the theological truth that undergirds verse 13 is to recognize that
sin always brings futility.

c. The Terror of Judgment (1:14–18). In what is perhaps
the most famous biblical description of the Day of the Lord,
Zephaniah tells of the imminent devastation, distress, and
darkness that dreadful day will bring to Judah.[8] The prophet
uses both supernatural and natural elements to describe the
terror and decimation. The brevity of the description makes it all
the more forceful. Especially striking are the five couplets in
verses 15 and 16a, which are better felt and experienced by the
reader rather than analyzed.

Hoping to lead his people to see the seriousness of the
situation, Zephaniah emphasizes the imminence and the bitterness of the day in verse 14. He returns to one of the themes of
verse 7, the nearness of the day. Now Zephaniah makes the
matter of imminence even more urgent by using the word
"near" twice and by using the phrase "coming quickly." In
addition, the word "near" is the first word of the verse; in
Hebrew syntax the first word is the most important element in
the sentence.

The last half of verse 14 is not as clear in meaning.
Commentators offer three major interpretations for it. Some
suggest the prophet is describing the skilled fighter's shout of
surprise and anguish on the Day of the Lord. This man suddenly
realizes that all of his training and ability are to no avail—he

---

[8]Zephaniah's dread prophecy found its fulfillment, at least in part, in the fall of
Judah to Babylon in 587 B.C. History has witnessed many "last days," all pointing
to that final "last day."

and his fellow citizens will be overrun by the judgment of that day. Others see the warrior as God Himself (see Isa. 42:13), who shouts the battle cry as He comes to judge.[9] Still others opt for a change in the reading of the Hebrew text, making the Day of the Lord swifter than the warrior. That is, it comes on him so quickly he cannot outrun it. Regardless of the interpretation one chooses, the thrust of the verse is that the Day of the Lord will be exceedingly bitter.

In verse 15 Zephaniah underscores the day as the outpouring of God's wrath. The Hebrew word translated "wrath" literally means "overflowing rage" or "fury." This should not be construed, however, as the uncontrolled temper of a capricious deity, who indiscriminately lashes out. A decidedly moral tone is struck here.

God's wrath is His tragic but inevitable response to Judah's rebellion. The people have sinned against the One who is righteous. Because of His very nature, God now moves to judge them. The "day of wrath" is the historical moment of His judgmental action.

The moral note is the key idea here, emphasized by the location of the phrase "a day of wrath" in the sentence. It occupies that initial spot of prominence mentioned earlier.

The four couplets that follow in verse 15 describe the effects of God's overflowing rage. A supernatural dimension seems to permeate the chilling terrors announced here. It is as if all of creation itself is in upheaval as God moves in judgment. Nature's convulsions serve to highlight God's self-revelation as He steps into history to judge Judah.

In addition to the supernatural dimension of the judgment, Zephaniah describes natural terrors (1:16). Judah will fall to a foreign military power, but the adversary's identity is not given. Such was of little importance to Zephaniah. He understood that the enemy army was Yahweh's agent.

---

[9]This interpretation is highly interesting, particularly in light of Isaiah's obvious influence on Zephaniah. Isaiah saw the Day of the Lord as a theophany, that is, God literally making an appearance on the stage of history. (Compare the statement of God *sitting* on the throne in Isaiah's call-experience in Isaiah 6:1 with Him *rising* to judge in Isaiah 3:13.) If Zephaniah envisions a similar idea, the passage before us graphically places God on the battlefield itself, breaking into the fabric of human history.

The sound of battle fills verse 16. The trumpet (a curved instrument generally made from a ram's horn) signaled troops' movements in combat. Battle cries frequently pierced the air in ancient warfare as a tactic to frighten prospective victims. Even Judah's "fortified cities" and "corner towers" (the battlements located on the corners of the city's walls) would be of no help in the onslaught.

The outer tragedy will produce inner turmoil for Judah's citizens (1:17). They will frantically search for ways to escape; their hopeless confusion will remind one of a blind man stumbling to find his way. The scene is one of agony. The people's blood (the symbol of life) will be poured out on the ground, thereby becoming as worthless to them as the dust with which it mingles. The last part of the verse ("their entrails like filth"), while interpreted in various ways, perhaps means that their dead bodies will be left where they fall in the slaughter. Left unburied, the mangled flesh will rot and decay. Again Zephaniah inserts the moral note: This terror comes "because they have sinned against the LORD."

The graphic description of the Day of the Lord closes in verse 18. Here Zephaniah reminds the people that they will not be able to buy their way out of judgment. The dread day is the occasion of God's wrath; it is the result of their sin.

While many commentators see in verse 18 a return to the universal judgment of Zephaniah 1:2–3, the context seems to speak against this. The prophet has clearly been dealing with Judah and Jerusalem since verse 4 and continues to do so through Zephaniah 2:3. The word translated "world" and "earth" in verse 18 also means "land." It probably refers to "the land of Judah." Thus Zephaniah declares that all of Judah's land and all who live in that land will be consumed by the fire of Yahweh's "jealousy."

d. The Shelter from Judgment (2:1–3). While numerous textual problems confront the interpreter of this section, the message seems clear. The great Day of the Lord is near. Before it strikes, however, the prophet's hearers have a possible chance to avert personal disaster. They are called on to seek a right relationship with God, and it just may be that within that relationship they "will be sheltered on the day of the LORD's anger."

The first problem here is contextual. Does Zephaniah 2:1–3 conclude the message to Judah begun in 1:4, or does it introduce the oracle against the Philistine nation in 2:4–7? Though some opt for the latter, their arguments seem weak and are rejected by most commentators.

Notice that the "shameful nation" of Zephaniah 2:1 is not called by name within this brief section. Could this be because Zephaniah had already identified Judah as the nation under discussion in 1:4? Would he abruptly change to the subject of Philistia (clearly identified for the first time in 2:4–7) without indicating what he was doing? It seems better to identify the shameful nation of 2:1 as Judah and to consider 2:1–3 as the conclusion to the sermon begun in chapter 1.[10]

Another difficulty revolves around the interpretation of the verb "gather together," which occurs twice in 2:1. Some grammarians suggest that the verb comes from the Hebrew word for "stubble" and thus means "to gather stubble." Various meanings have been suggested for the present context. Some propose the verb suggests people being summoned "to assemble."

Other scholars view the word as a call for spiritual self-examination and translate it as "collect yourselves." This position underscores that repentance and spiritual transformation never come without one's awareness of personal sin and need in the presence of God. Thus Zephaniah is calling on the people to take the first step to conversion. Still others, noting that the gathering of stubble is backbreaking work, translate the verb as "bend yourselves," emphasizing the need for the Judeans to stoop in humility before God.

Yet another problem is presented by the Hebrew text of verse 2. The literal reading is extremely difficult, leading commentators to suggest various textual changes. Be that as it may, the verse emphasizes the reason why Zephaniah now issues the call to right relationship with God. The prophet's tone

---

[10] Identification of Judah as the "nation" is important in Zephaniah's message. The Hebrew word the prophet used here was generally used for foreign or heathen nations; another word—the "people"—was the usual designation for Judah. By using "nation" for Judah, Zephaniah declared that the covenant people had identified with the world rather than with God. They were no longer unique; they were merely one among the many heathen nations of the world.

is urgent. The great day is imminent. The shameful nation will soon experience judgment. If Zephaniah's hearers are to have any chance at all, they must act soon; it will be too late to repent when the day of wrath arrives.

Verse 3 reveals the demands of the prophet's urgent call. The people are to "seek the LORD," that is, they are to form a living, vital relationship with God. Such a relationship only comes when people are willing to humble themselves before God, recognize their sinfulness, and turn in repentance to Him. Life in this relationship is to be lived in righteousness (their acts must reflect the very righteousness of God as revealed by His Law) and in humility (their attitudes must reflect submission and obedience to God).

Only in such living is there even a chance the Judeans might be saved on the Day of the Lord. That Zephaniah holds out no promise for survival on that day is confirmed by his use of the word "perhaps" (also translated "it may be") in the concluding comment of verse 3. "Perhaps" those who seek the Lord "will be sheltered on the day of the LORD's anger." In other words, when the great day devastates Judah, some of the righteous may be spared the terrors while others of them may in fact suffer. Thus in a book that has been negative from the start, we see the first glimmer of hope. Zephaniah will develop that hope more fully in passages to come.

2. *The Judgment of Judah's Neighbors (2:4–15)*

Sermons against foreign nations are common in the Old Testament prophetic books. That is not surprising because certain basic theological concepts are foundational to such preaching. God is not simply the God of Israel; He is the sovereign ruler of all humanity. People everywhere are subject to His moral law. Human sin, wherever it occurs, merits judgment. And even as the prophetic outlook on judgment was universal, so also was the prophetic hope for the future.

Zephaniah follows the example of other prophets with his own series of sermons against foreign nations. The theological concepts mentioned above find expression in his preaching. And yet in a sense, Zephaniah's foreign sermons reinforce that his *major* concern was with his own nation. The locations of the nations he cites are significant: (1) Philistia (2:4–7) on the west of Judah; (2) Moab and Ammon (2:8–11) on the east; (3) Cush (2:12) on the south; and (4) Assyria (2:13–15) on the north. In the very center of these places was Judah! While the listing of sites east, west, north, and south on the one hand affirms the universality of the judgment, it also puts the focus on Judah. Zephaniah's hearers would understand that the nations mentioned represent the whole world, but they would also see Judah on center stage.

Furthermore, Zephaniah says little about the sins of these other nations. Was this a deliberate move to focus even more clearly on Judah's sinfulness?

Surely the brief but important sermons of this section magnify God's universal rule. But since these messages were heard primarily by Judeans, their underlying purpose seems obvious: they were amplifications of Judah's sin and certain judgment.

a. The Judgment of Philistia (2:4–7). Zephaniah's word about Philistia is totally negative. Four significant Philistine cities are singled out for depopulation and destruction (2:4). It is a common opinion that Zephaniah intended the four to represent the entire nation.

Our English translations fail to reflect the striking Hebrew original of this verse. Once again Zephaniah uses the paronomastic device (using words of a similar sound to create an effect, like a pun), which is frequently found in the prophets. The Hebrew words for "Gaza" and "abandoned" sound much alike, as do those for "Ekron" and "uprooted." It has also been suggested that the verb rendered "emptied" by the NIV is a deliberate pun on the name "Ashdod."

The order in which the four cities are mentioned may provide an interesting insight into Zephaniah's purpose. Gaza, the southernmost city, is mentioned first; it is about fifty miles from Jerusalem. Ashkelon, mentioned next, is twelve miles north of Gaza. Ashdod, twenty-one miles from Gaza, and Ekron, the northernmost city another twelve miles away, follow. Is the movement of destruction from Gaza ever closer to Jerusalem yet another clue to Zephaniah's predominant concern with Judah?

In verse 5 Zephaniah announces the prophetic "woe" of

final judgment to the Philistines, who are identified as the "Kerethite people." Scholars debate the meaning of the word "Kerethite." Most scholars conclude that either it is the name of a major Philistine clan that lived on the coast or it is somehow connected with Crete, thought by many to be the original home of the Philistines. The word might refer to an otherwise unidentified city named Kerith.

The most interesting proposal is that Zephaniah used the word as a pun. "Kerethite" is related to a verbal form meaning "to cut off, exterminate." On the one hand, the word would signify the Philistines as "cutters" or "exterminators" (who took what they wanted by force); but on the other hand, it would indicate that they themselves would be "cut off."

The prophet gives no reason for Philistia's fate. He simply announces that "the word of the LORD" was against the nation. This declaration of divine judgment, without mention of any prior sin, should not lead one to characterize God as a capricious deity who strikes without justification. Philistia's long history of paganism, though not mentioned by Zephaniah, is well documented.

The destruction of Philistia will be total. "None will be left" (2:5). The sophisticated and cultured Philistine cities will be replaced by pasture lands fit only for nomads (2:6). The accuracy of Zephaniah's prediction is evident today; the Philistines are a forgotten people, with only isolated names like Delilah and Goliath to remind us that they ever existed.

In verse 7 Zephaniah turns from Philistia's destruction to the future of its former territory. That land, fit for shepherds, would one day be occupied by "the remnant of the house of Judah." Here is another glimmer of hope in the prophet's bleak message. He envisions an ideal future, after the great Day of the Lord, when Judah's righteous would know God's unique blessings. In the land of their ancient enemy, they would "find pasture." In the house of Ashkelon, they would sleep securely under the watchful care of "their God." He would "restore their fortunes."

The last comment in verse 7 has caused some difficulty. The Hebrew literally reads: "And he will turn away their captivity." Zephaniah may be thinking of the release from the Babylonian exile, nearly a century away. Or he may be using a metaphorical idiom reflecting general, future blessing. Regardless of one's view, the verse represents a genuine hopeful note for those who "seek the Lord."

b. The Judgment of Moab and Ammon (2:8–11). Zephaniah next turns his attention to Judah's geographical east, to the Transjordanian nations of Moab and Ammon. These peoples were blood relatives of Judah, coming from Lot's incestuous union with his daughters (see Gen. 19:30–38). Conflicts between the Judeans and these two neighboring states were frequent over the centuries.

As this section begins, God Himself speaks. He cites sins of Moab and Ammon. They are guilty of taunting God's people (and thus God Himself) with arrogant verbal abuse and of encroaching on Judean territory (2:8).[11]

The exact historical occasion Zephaniah had in mind is impossible to identify. In fact he may not even have pinpointed one specific incident. Rather he may have surveyed the long history of bad relations between Judah and these two eastern neighbors and then summarized the consistent Moabite-Ammonite attitude.

In verse 9 God announces the judgment that will come to Moab and Ammon because of their sin. The complete certainty of the judgment is confirmed by the oath that God takes on His very existence ("as surely as I live").

Two aspects of the judgment are revealed. First, Moab and Ammon will be destroyed even as were ancient Sodom and Gomorrah (see Gen. 19:24–25). Their land will become "a place of weeds and salt pits, a wasteland forever."

Zephaniah's use of Sodom and Gomorrah, a common biblical symbol for total destruction, was especially appropriate in this case. These ancient cities were located in the same general region as Moab and Ammon. Sodom and Gomorrah were also used as symbols for wickedness in the Old Testament (see Isa. 1:10; Jer. 23:14); perhaps Zephaniah also intended this meaning.

The second aspect of judgment contains yet another brief

---

[11] In light of Deuteronomy 32:8, Ammonite and Moabite invasions of Judah were sins against God.

glimmer of hope for Judah's righteous remnant. As they would one day possess Philistine territory, so also would they "plunder" and "inherit" the lands of Moab and Ammon (2:9). Some commentators have seen an inconsistency because the land was to be destroyed on the one hand and absorbed by Judah on the other. Such need not be a problem, however. Both aspects of the judgment signify the same end: Moab and Ammon will be no more!

Verse 10 emphatically summarizes the preceding verses. "This" (the destruction and absorption) is what Moab and Ammon will receive for their proud, arrogant behavior. One cannot help but recall another biblical passage: "Pride goes before destruction, a haughty spirit before a fall" (Prov. 16:18; see also Prov. 18:12).

Having now commented on neighbors west and east, Zephaniah is ready to touch the other two compass points. But before he does, he pauses in verse 11 to reveal the purpose of God's judgments in the pagan world. This verse is one of the great passages of the Bible. By destroying the gods of the nations, God will lead people everywhere to recognize that He alone is sovereign Lord. All nations will then seek Him and worship Him even in their own lands. With these magnificent words, Zephaniah expresses a universal hope. Not only does Judah's remnant have a future, but all those in the world who put their trust in Him as true God will also have a future.

c. The Judgment of Cush (2:12). The southern neighbor, Cush (or Ethiopia), receives only brief notice. Located south of Egypt, Cush for a time had ruled its great northern neighbor. Egypt's Twenty-fifth Dynasty had been Ethiopian. It had lost power about 660 B.C., only a few years before Zephaniah's ministry.

Many commentators, therefore, identify Cush with Egypt here, suggesting that Zephaniah called the Egyptians "Cushites" as a taunt. Others do not share this view. They contend Zephaniah mentioned Cush because it was farther south than any other nation known to Judah. Though the exact identification of Cush here may never be resolved, the sermon's point is obvious: nations in the south, like those in the east and west, would experience God's judgment.

d. The Judgment of Assyria (2:13–15). Zephaniah turns finally to the north, the fourth compass point, and singles out Assyria with its capital city Nineveh. This great, cruel power had ruled the ancient world for decades with iron-handed domination. By saving the obvious worst for last, Zephaniah brings his series of foreign sermons to a strong climax.

The scene in these three verses is graphic.[12] God's out-stretched hand will leave Nineveh devastated and desolate, an uninhabited wilderness on a desertlike landscape. Wild creatures will make their homes in the ruins of the great palaces and buildings of state. Rubble and rubbish, tragic reminders of judgment, will cover the area. Cries of wild birds will reverberate through the ruins. Beautiful panels of cedar that graced the palaces' inner chambers in better days will be exposed to weather and beast.

Why such destruction for Nineveh? This proud city that thought so well of itself, that considered itself invincible ("the carefree city that lived in safety"), had tried to deify itself. Its very words contend that it is without equal: "She said to herself, 'I am, and there is none besides me'" (2:15). These words claim a status of absolute power and complete independence that in no way properly characterizes finite humanity. These words can only be descriptive of God and are in fact somewhat parallel to His self-characterization in Isaiah 45 (see verses 5, 6, 18, and 21). Yet Nineveh made those words a personal identification. Such arrogant, self-centered blasphemy can only lead to ruin.

Zephaniah concludes his brief oracle on Nineveh with words similar to the final verse in Nahum. Those who pass by the desolate city "scoff and shake their fists" in utter contempt and hatred. Victimized by the notorious city, they can only believe that Nineveh got exactly what it deserved.

---

[12] The first two verses are predictive, whereas verse 15 seems to have been written after Nineveh's fall in 612 B.C. It is often difficult to determine time-orientation in Hebrew verbs. Perhaps verse 15 should also be interpreted as prediction. Or it may be that Zephaniah added the verse after Nineveh's fall as an illustration of God accomplishing in history what He declared He would do.

3. A Reiteration of Judgment on Jerusalem and the Nations (3:1–8)

With chapter 3 Zephaniah returns to the situation in Jerusalem in his own day.[13] His first word, the prophetic "woe" of final judgment, indicates that few have responded to his earlier invitation to "seek the LORD" (2:3). Instead, the scene is one of widespread moral and spiritual degeneracy. Both the people at large and the various classes of leadership are guilty.

The prophet begins an indictment against the general population by characterizing Jerusalem as "the city of oppressors, rebellious and defiled" (3:1). The order of these descriptive words differs in Hebrew, where "rebellious" comes first. This word, which can also be rendered "defiant," in the Old Testament often expresses a stubborn refusal to follow God's way. It describes the people's attitude toward God. Next is the word "defiled" or "polluted." It refers to the inner character of the people, which has been affected by their many sins. The third word is "oppressors," which describes the cruel actions against others.

The Hebrew order of these words serves to illustrate the way sin works. Sin is *rebellion* against God that *pollutes* or *defiles* the very being of the sinner, who then strikes out by *oppressing* others.

The indictment against the people continues in verse 2, where four specific charges are made:

(1) "She obeys no one." The Hebrew literally reads: "She listened not to a voice." The "voice" is generally thought to be God's as expressed in the Law or in prophetic preaching.

(2) "She accepts no correction." This statement either means that the people did not learn from the chastisements God sent them (see Amos 4:6–11) or if "correction" is understood as "instruction," that they did not heed God's guidance for living.

(3) "She does not trust in the LORD." The arrangement of this sentence in Hebrew is instructive. The prepositional phrase "in the LORD" comes first and thus should have the emphasis in interpretation. "*In the LORD* she does not trust." Jerusalem's

---

[13] Jerusalem is never named in Zephaniah 3:1–8. It is clear, however, from the context that the city is meant (consider, for example, the reference to the law in verse 4).

faith should have been in no one but the Lord, yet in reality the people put their faith in everyone and everything *but* Him. (For example, they trusted in alliances with other nations, in idols, in military power.)

(4) "She does not draw near to her God." Again the Hebrew places the prepositional phrase at the beginning of the sentence. "To her God" Jerusalem's citizens should have turned in penitent worship, but He was far from their minds.

Having listed the charges against the people, Zephaniah next focuses on the political, judicial, and religious leadership of the land (3:3–4). These especially should have been sensitive to God's place in Judean life; their failure is thereby all the more acute.

Political leaders, both the "officials" who daily administer the government and the "rulers" or judges who administer justice, are compared to beasts of prey that devour as quickly as they can ("who leave nothing for the morning"). They use their positions for personal gain, corrupting the government and destroying the very people they were to shepherd.

The religious leaders are no better. The prophets, for example, are "arrogant." The Hebrew verbal root from which this word comes means "to boil over," which gives the idea of "unrestrained," "reckless," or "boiling over with frivolous words." In other words, these prophets speak trivial, self-centered words from their own imagination and try to pass them off as God's message. They are "treacherous men," which probably indicates their personal rebellion against the God they supposedly serve.

The priests handle holy things with a lack of reverence. They are unable to distinguish between sacred and profane, thus profaning that which is holy. They also "do violence to the law," both by misinterpreting it to the people and by failing personally to live by its standards.

In stark contrast to Jerusalem's sinfulness is the example of Yahweh (3:5). He dwells in the city, always faithful to demonstrate the right way, never failing to reveal what He requires. But even that perfect example is not enough for Jerusalem's unrighteous. They "know no shame" for their sin; they refuse to seek the Lord.

In verse 6 God becomes the speaker once again. This sudden shift of speakers is a common feature in the prophets. Here God describes His past actions of judgment on other nations. No identification of these nations is given nor is one necessary. The point is that Jerusalem should learn from history that sin brings judgment. What happened to others will happen also to Jerusalem.

Verse 7 continues God's speech. Significant here are the Hebrew verbs, which are designed to express God's deep wish. He had hoped that His acts of judgment on other nations (like those mentioned in verse 6) and the chastisements on Judah would have led Jerusalem to "fear" (that is, to have faith in, reverence for) Him. If that had been the case, Jerusalem would not have been destroyed. But tragically, Jerusalem's sinners were so degenerate that they shrugged off such gracious warnings and sinned with even greater eagerness.

Because all of God's invitations fell on deaf ears, judgment is inevitable. Verse 8 again picks up the central theme of the Day of the Lord, identifying it as "the day I will stand up to testify" or "witness." God's witness will be against the wicked in both Judah and the nations.

The divine witness is also the judge. He will "assemble the nations" and "gather the kingdoms" to "pour out" His "wrath on them." The verse closes with a return to the note of universal judgment with which the message was introduced in 1:2–3: "The whole world will be consumed by the fire of my jealous anger."

This grave conclusion contains a note of hope. To the few pious, God instructs: "wait for me."[14] These words point them beyond the tragedy of the Day of the Lord to the glorious future that will follow. The believers are to trust God, confident that He will see them through the judgment to the glad day of restoration.

---

[14]Some commentators see God's words here as ironic and threatening, similar to Amos 4:12. Most, however, see the instruction as positive.

Chapter 9

The Glad Day of Restoration
(Zephaniah 3:9–20)

The long opening sermon of Zephaniah (1:2–3:8) is very bleak. The dark Day of the Lord with its judgmental dimension is described in vivid detail. Positive words are few and far between.

The first positive glimmer comes in Zephaniah 2:3. There the prophet offers the hope, but no promise, that those who seek the Lord might be saved from the terrors of the day of wrath. "Perhaps you will be sheltered," he says.

Another glimmer of hope comes in 2:7, where Judah's remnant is accepted as a reality. Some people indeed *would* be saved from the judgment, and in the period following the Day of the Lord, they would occupy the land of their ancient enemies, the Philistines. A similar note of hope comes in 2:9 with the remnant's claim to Moabite and Ammonite territory, though this passage is not as detailed as 2:7.

The next positive word comes in 2:11. It is significant, for it reveals that some people from among the Gentile nations would also be saved from the tragic day. Furthermore, in the future they would worship Yahweh.

The long sermon begins to shift from the negative to the positive in its last four verses (3:5–8). Though the major emphasis here is still on the Day of the Lord as a day of universal judgment, glimmers of hope are evident in each verse.

In verse 5 the prophet told Jerusalem that God, living in the city's midst, had attempted to show the people the right way. He had hoped that judgments of other nations would warn them (verse 6). God's agonizing for Jerusalem is revealed in verse 7. And finally in verse 8 God encourages the faithful few with the words "wait for me." This brief instruction points the believer to a glorious future after the tragedy of the Day of the Lord.

As we come now to the concluding sermon of Zephaniah's book, we find an attitude totally different from that of the earlier sermon. Here the prophet's words soar with enthusiasm and joy as he describes the glad day of restoration.[1]

The final message is divided into four parts: (A) The Nations' Restoration (3:9–10); (B) Jerusalem's Restoration (3:11–13); (C) Joy's Restoration (3:14–17); and (D) The Diaspora's Restoration (3:18–20).

A. The Nations' Restoration (3:9–10)

The initial words of verse 9 link this new sermon with what has gone before: "Then will I purify the lips of the peoples." The Hebrew literally reads: "For then will I turn (restore, change) to the peoples a pure lip." The phrase "for then" refers to the Day of the Lord mentioned previously, specifically in 3:8.

The earlier glimmers of hope now begin to brighten. It becomes clear that the purpose of the Day of the Lord is not simply the destruction described so vividly in 1:2–3:8. The terrible day has a constructive purpose as well; it will be a time for purification and restoration.

The Hebrew reading of this verse suggests the idea of change initiated by God, who is the speaker in this section. He declares that He will "turn" the lip of the peoples (that is, the nations of the world). Based on a comparison with 1 Samuel 10:9 (where the same verb is used), the idea here seems to be that God will graciously change the impure lip into a pure lip.

Purifying the lip may involve a twofold emphasis. In this connection commentators divide rather evenly in their conclusions about the two options. The key to the discussion is the meaning given to the word "lips," which is actually singular in Hebrew. Does this word refer to the "language" or the "inner

---

[1]The eschatology of the Old Testament prophets had three basic points: (1) The world in which they lived was totally corrupt. (2) God would act in judgment against the fallen world. (3) A glorious golden age would follow the judgment. Zephaniah's book certainly reflects this basic eschatological pattern.

life and personality" of the peoples? In other words, is the issue here unity of speech or purity of heart?

If the latter is the issue, Zephaniah may have had in mind some passage like Isaiah's call-experience. Isaiah had identified himself as a sinner, a "man of unclean lips" (Isa. 6:5). His confession revealed an inner being far from God, manifested by impure words and lip service. By God's gracious forgiving action, Isaiah was cleansed, given a purified life and clean lips. Zephaniah may have envisioned this kind of experience for the people of the world in the golden age.

If, on the other hand, the prophet had in mind unity of speech, he may have been reflecting on the ancient story of Babel (see Gen. 11:1–9). There God confused humanity's language because the people lived in rebellion against Him. Zephaniah's emphasis would thus be that God will give a "purified language" or common tongue so that all might communicate together in their common and shared worship of Him. Babel's judgment would thus be reversed in the restoration.

The first of the two options may be the better interpretation. Certainly we have seen Isaiah's influence on Zephaniah. Also a gift of unified speech really cannot be conceived apart from an initial change of life.

And yet the emphasis on unified speech should not be discounted. The remainder of the verse certainly emphasizes unified worship ("that all of them may call on the name of the LORD") and unified service ("serve him shoulder to shoulder").

Verse 10 continues the emphasis of unified worship. Its exact content, however, is quite debatable; the Hebrew is very difficult to translate.

The phrase "from beyond the rivers of Cush" is meant to convey the idea of remoteness. Cush was the southernmost nation known to Zephaniah's Judah. Thus the expression designates those who worship God in the most distant places of the earth. These "scattered people" bring Him "offerings."

But who are the scattered people? And what are their offerings? Three interpretations (none of which can be verified) have been suggested. (1) Some commentators interpret here a reference to the Gentiles, scattered abroad in the world by their sin (see Isa. 18:7; 45:14; John 11:51–52). The Gentiles will bring God offerings (pay homage to Him), not necessarily by going to Jerusalem, but in their own lands (see Zeph. 2:11).

(2) Others see the scattered people as Judeans, dispersed by the Day of the Lord. They will return to Jerusalem, either giving themselves as an offering to God or participating again in the Old Testament sacrificial system.

(3) Still other commentators compare the passage to Isaiah 66:20. They conclude that the worshipers are Gentiles who bring dispersed Judeans back to their land as an offering to God in gratitude for what He has done for them. By bringing the chosen people home, the Gentiles demonstrate their own conversion.

The Hebrew text is much too uncertain to be dogmatic about any of these interpretations. But the two verses do emphasize God's gracious action in restoring citizens of the world to Him. They will be purified in life and thus unified in language, worship, and service. This ideal occurrence will be realized, according to Zephaniah, in that glorious period following the Day of the Lord.

B. Jerusalem's Restoration (3:11–13)

Again in this section God is the speaker. He addresses His message to Jerusalem. A remarkable contrast is drawn between the Jerusalem of Zephaniah's day (see 1:4–13; 3:1–8) and the Jerusalem that will be (3:11–13). The two cities are exact opposites. The one, "rebellious and defiled" (3:1), will be consumed with the rest of the world (3:8). The other—the new Jerusalem—will be purified and restored to God's favor.

This amazing transformation will occur "on that day" (3:11). This phrase, which earlier referred to the Day of the Lord (see 1:10, for example), is expanded in this context. Here it refers both to the Day of the Lord and to the glorious golden age that follows it.

The restored city "will not be put to shame" for its wrongs against God (3:11). Some commentators interpret Zephaniah to mean that Jerusalem will simply forget past sins. The context, however, seems to suggest that there will be no future shame because those responsible for past sins will be removed in the judgment.

In discussing Jerusalem's purification, Zephaniah is especially concerned with the sin of pride, particularly among the religious leadership (see 3:4). In the new city, none who are haughty will be "on my holy hill," which refers to Mount Zion, the temple, and the official religious practice of Jerusalem.

The citizens of the restored Jerusalem are described in verses 12 and 13. They are "the meek and humble," those "who trust in [take refuge in] the name of the LORD." Such trust is the essential biblical requirement for fellowship with God.

This "remnant" community "will do no wrong"; rather they will imitate the righteous God they serve. "They will speak no lies, nor will deceit be found in their mouths." This passage suggests, in embryonic fashion, the concept of regeneration as later developed in the New Testament.

The passage closes with a peaceful scene of pastoral security. With imagery taken from the shepherd's vocabulary, Zephaniah declares that the remnant will be provided food, rest, and protection. No one will harm them. Trusting in their God, they can be confident of His watchful care (see 2:7). Zephaniah has taken us a long way from the grim scenes found in the book's long opening sermon.

C. Joy's Restoration (3:14–17)

Judean exiles in Babylon several decades after Zephaniah expressed their despair in a moving psalm: "By the rivers of Babylon we sat and wept when we remembered Zion. There on the poplars we hung our harps, for there our captors asked us for songs, our tormentors demanded songs of joy; they said, 'Sing us one of the songs of Zion!' How can we sing the songs of the LORD while in a foreign land?" (Ps. 137:1–4).

In the present passage Zephaniah continues to look beyond the judgment to future restoration. It is to be a restoration of joy and, consequently, of song.

In verse 14 the prophet bids his people to sing. Three titles are used for the restored remnant; three different expressions are used for the call to worship. These threefold repetitions emphasize the occasion's uniqueness. How marvelous is Judah's new opportunity! How grateful the nation should be to God! It should demonstrate its joy enthusiastically in songs of praise!

Verse 15 presents four specific reasons for joy. (1) "The LORD has taken away your punishment." All judgments inflicted on Judah for its sin are removed; sin is pardoned (see also Isa. 40:2). (2) "He has turned back your enemy." The various agents that were instrumental in the judgments are swept away. The verb Zephaniah uses here has the connotation of putting something in order by removing or "turning out" that which causes disorder. (3) "The LORD, the King of Israel, is with you." Here is the great promise of God's presence, a promise made so often in the Bible. God's presence emphasizes intimacy of fellowship and communion with Him, as well as safety and prosperity. (4) "Never again will you fear any harm." The LXX changes the verb "fear" to "see" (that is, "experience"). There is little difference in the Hebrew words involved, and today most scholars accept the LXX reading.

Referring again to "that day" in verse 16, Zephaniah underscores the new attitude that should characterize the remnant community. No longer should they fear or stand defeated in despair ("do not let your hands hang limp"). Fear and despondency are the opposites of faith and joy and thus have no place in the lives of the redeemed. They are to be a joyful people.

Why should they be? The reason is evident: "The LORD your God is with you, he is mighty to save" (3:17). Here the great promise of verse 15 is reiterated, but with a new thought added. The present God is mighty (a "warrior," a "hero"), with the ability "to save." He is the One who provides salvation. Is that not one more reason for the redeemed remnant to rejoice?

At this point the emphasis suddenly changes. With three striking statements,[2] Zephaniah tells of God's joy over His people. These bold anthropomorphisms describe God's inner

---

[2] The middle statement ("He will quiet you with his love") occasions some difficulty for interpreters. The Hebrew literally reads: "He will be silent in His love." The LXX changes the emphasis to: "He will renew (refresh) you with His love." Some scholars interpret the Hebrew to mean that God remains silent about the remnant's sin, never bringing it before them because it is forgiven. This idea seems totally foreign to the context. Perhaps the best position is that the statement describes a depth of love that cannot express itself; this is contrasted then, paradoxically, with a deep love that issues forth in joyful song. The paradoxical combination thus magnifies the intensity of God's love for the redeemed.

delight and satisfaction in His people; this satisfaction eventually issues forth in a burst of glad song. How moving is the thought of God singing His joy over His redeemed people! Surely the greatest reason for them to offer praise is found here. They are to rejoice in Him because He, their gracious King and Savior, rejoices in them. Those who see the Old Testament as harsh and forbidding have not given proper attention to passages like this.

D. The Diaspora's Restoration (3:18–20)

The Hebrew in this section is difficult, nowhere more so than in verse 18. The LXX attempts to solve the problems by placing the first two words of the Hebrew text at the end of verse 17. With that change, verse 17 describes God's rejoicing over His people "as on a day of festival [feasting]," whereas verse 18 reveals that God will "gather" those who are afflicted.

Perhaps it is better to leave the reference to the "appointed feasts" in verse 18 and to suggest the following approach. The exiled Judeans are sorrowful because they cannot participate in the religious observance in Jerusalem. God, therefore, promises to "remove" these sorrows, which "are a burden and a reproach" to them. This promise is the first of six in the sermon's concluding section.

In verse 19 three additional promises are given. First, God "will deal with all who oppressed" His people. The verb rendered "deal with" can be either negative or positive. The former usage is obvious here. Those responsible for Judah's afflictions will be rendered ineffective.

This action paves the way for the next promise. God "will rescue the lame and gather those who have been scattered." These images from the shepherd's realm refer to the plight of the homeless, crippled Judeans, banished from their land to the distant places of the earth. God, the faithful Shepherd, will seek and recover them. He will bring the fold together once again.

Furthermore, He promises to "give them praise and honor." Their reputations had suffered badly in their defeat and exile, but now their significance as a people would be accepted in the lands "where they were put to shame."

The final verse of the sermon is in part repetitious. It again affirms that God will locate the outcast Judeans ("at that time I will gather you"). Added here is the fifth great promise of the passage: God "will bring" them "home." The exile will end. The dispersed Judeans will again walk Jerusalem's streets.

Zephaniah then repeats the good word that Judah's place of honor among the nations will be confirmed. He expands the idea with the sixth promise of the passage. The confirmation of fame will come when God restores their "fortunes." To nail down the certainty of the promise with finality, Zephaniah adds that this will happen "before your very eyes." This idiom seems to be equivalent to the idea of "most definitely" or "it will be"; in other words, this turn in events will "certainly happen."

The book closes on a dramatic note. The last two words in the Hebrew text are, "said Yahweh." The certainty of the message is reaffirmed. These are not a man's promises; these are the words of Yahweh Himself.[3] When Yahweh determines to do a work, who can stop Him?

For Further Study on Zephaniah

1. Zephaniah describes the destruction of nature on the day of universal judgment in 1:2–3. Some commentators criticize the prophet for failing to predict the restoration of nature. How would you respond to this criticism?

2. Was Zephaniah's concept of the Day of the Lord fully realized in Jerusalem's fall to Babylon in 587 B.C.? Are there many Days of the Lord? Is there one great Day of the Lord? Support your answers from Scripture.

3. Reread Zephaniah 1:12. In what specific ways could this passage be descriptive of the church today? Of our culture?

4. On a map of the biblical world find: (a) the five nations mentioned in Zephaniah 2:4–15; (b) the four cities mentioned in 2:4; (c) the supposed location of Sodom and Gomorrah (2:9).

5. In light of the Old Testament relationship to the New Testament, how do you understand passages like Zephaniah 3:9–20? Are the promises fulfilled in the Christian church? What significance is there in this passage for the Jewish people today?

---

[3] Notice the number of "I's" in reference to Yahweh in 3:18–20.

6. Reread Zephaniah 3:9. Consider again the emphasis on the "pure lip." What connection do you see between this passage and Acts 2?

7. Study the concept of "remnant" in several Bible dictionaries.

8. Read Alexander Maclaren's marvelous sermon on Zephaniah 3:14–17 entitled "Zion's Joy and God's" in his series of books *Maclaren's Expositions of Holy Scripture* (William B. Eerdman's Publishing Company).

9. Reread the promises in Zephaniah 3:19. Notice that God promised to give the redeemed remnant "praise and honor." Consider the following questions: (a) Does Zephaniah imply that God will be honored through the praise bestowed on the people? (b) Is there an echo here of God's promise to make Abraham famous (see Gen. 12:2)? (c) If the age of restoration envisioned by the prophets is the New Testament era (as many believe), in what way is Israel now praised? Is Christ's coming from Israel the ultimate fulfillment of Zephaniah's promise?

Chapter 10

An Introduction to Haggai and His Prophecy

Haggai was the first prophet in the period of the restoration. The situation in Judah had changed drastically from pre-exilic days. The people previously were caught up in the whirl of religious activity, going through external motions without any regard for a right relationship with God. It had been a day of religion for religion's sake. Pre-exilic prophets like Jeremiah had warned that the temple and the external religious practices in which the people put their faith would be destroyed.

And such dire predictions had come to pass. Jerusalem had fallen. The temple had been leveled. Judah's finest people had been exiled to Babylon.

But now it is a new day. Release from the Babylonian captivity has finally come. Some of the Judeans returned to their homeland about 537 B.C. But early efforts to rebuild the temple had stalled, and for more than fifteen years the temple ruins were left in disrepair. The people showed little real interest in the temple or religious affairs. Rather they showed indifference and apathy to the things of God. Concern focused only on trying to survive and carve out a new life in a land sorely in need of reconstruction. Selfish preoccupation was the order of the day.

Recognizing the temple's vital significance for the faith of Judah, Haggai appeared briefly in 520 B.C. and hammered home the need for its reconstruction. But it is unfair to credit this prophet merely with the task of rebuilding a ruined structure. Profound spiritual issues are the foundation of his preaching. Haggai was God's man of the moment, chosen to call an indifferent people to spiritual responsibility. The rebuilding of the temple represented a far deeper issue than a building campaign; the temple symbolized God's presence with His people. The refusal to reconstruct the temple revealed the disrespect the people held for God. They blatantly broadcast their lack of faith in His presence by making no provision for Him to dwell in their midst. In Haggai's view, this spiritual indifference was the sole cause for the troubles the struggling community faced. To rebuild the temple was to respond unequivocally in faith to God.

Furthermore, as we will see, the temple's reconstruction had eschatological overtones for Haggai. It was the starting place, a sign of hope, for a greater restoration for God's people in the future. It is a tragedy that contemporary readers pass by this little book with the impression that it has no value; nothing could be further from the truth.

A. Haggai the Man

Information about Haggai's personal history is virtually nonexistent. He is mentioned only in the book that bears his name and in Ezra 5:1–2 and 6:14. Nowhere do we have any information about his family. This lack of genealogical record may suggest humble origins. A number of Jewish and Christian traditions exist about his life, but these are without historical verification. What little we know of Haggai must be ascertained from his brief book. One thing is certain: he was privileged like few other prophets in that he saw positive results of his labor.

1. Haggai's Name

No one in the Old Testament except this prophet bears the name Haggai, although a son of Gad is called Haggi (see Gen. 46:16; Num. 26:15). The only difference between the latter and the prophet's name is a Hebrew vowel point. Since vowel points were added to the Hebrew text long after the Old Testament era, the original name of the two men may have been the same. In the LXX the prophet's name is Aggaios, while in the Vulgate it is Haggaeus or Aggaeus.

Evidently the name Haggai derives from the Hebrew word for "feast" or "festival." Thus "Haggai" itself means "festal" or "festive," connoting joy. It is generally assumed that he was so named because he was born on or near the time of one of the great Israelite festivals.

Some commentators contend that Haggai is an abbreviated form of Haggiah, which means "the feast of Yahweh" (see 1 Chron. 6:30). Still others suggest the name is a possible contraction of Hagariah, which means "Yahweh girds." Similar names have been found in ancient Aramaic and Phoenician materials.

One view that seems to have been put to rest is that Haggai is not a personal name but a title for an otherwise anonymous book. The book was supposedly called "Haggai" or "my feasts" because the sermons contained therein were preached on festival days. This position has had little support, primarily because the last two sermons were preached on a day in which there was no known festival (see Hag. 2:10, 20).

If the name is a clue to Haggai's life or ministry, it perhaps underscores his joy in seeing his people respond to his preaching. It may be, as several scholars have said, the name is a sign of the faith of Haggai's parents. They recognized that God would use their son in joyous ministry and thus named him "festive" or "the exuberant one."

2. Haggai's Home

Jerusalem was the site of Haggai's ministry, at least as his work is reflected in his book. But to say more goes beyond the realm of verification. Was he born in Babylon during the exile, returning to Jerusalem for his ministry? Had he preached some in Babylon? Do his probable humble origins suggest that his family was left behind in the deportation, that he was born in Jerusalem (or Judah), and that he remained there all his life? Despite various traditions, such questions have no answers. We are only able to locate Haggai for a few months in Jerusalem.

3. Haggai's Date

Certain dates in Haggai's story can be given with a precision not seen in our studies of Nahum, Habakkuk, and Zephaniah. Other dates are totally lacking.

From the positive side, the precise year of Haggai's ministry was 520 B.C., which was the second year in the reign of Darius of Persia. Each recorded sermon is dated as to month and even day. For example the first sermon came "on the first day of the sixth month" (Hag. 1:1). A synchronization of the calendar used in Haggai with the Julian calendar identifies the day of the first sermon as August 29, 520 B.C. The last two sermons were delivered "on the twenty-fourth day of the ninth month" (Hag. 2:10, 20), which was December 18 of the same year. Thus Haggai's ministry—as recorded in his book—spanned less than four months in 520 B.C.

But other dates are unavailable. For example, when was Haggai born? Some commentators believe he was born in Judah prior to Jerusalem's fall, making him some eighty years old when he preached. The brevity of his recorded ministry supports this view, it is argued. Others contend he was born during the Babylonian captivity and was a young man when he preached in Jerusalem. The truth is that we simply have no way of knowing his birth date, the date of his call-experience, his age at the time of his recorded ministry, the length of his ministry, whether he lived to see the new temple complete, or the date of his death.

4. Haggai's Occupation

Several ancient traditions associate Haggai with the priesthood. One from Hesychius indicates that he was of priestly lineage. Some of the versions suggest he was the author of several psalms, evidently reflecting his purported role in the worship of the second temple.[1] Some commentators today point to his concern for temple restoration and his appeal to the priesthood in 2:10–19 as internal clues of his priestly vocation.

However, none of the evidence is conclusive. Haggai's interest in temple restoration has vital theological ramifications; he is not simply calling for a return to temple ritual. Also his appeal to the priests in 2:10–19 appears to reveal he was outside their number rather than among them. In short, no real evidence identifies Haggai as either a priest or a prophet connected to the religious establishments. His occupation is another of the unknowns about his life.

---

[1] The versions and respective psalms are: (1) LXX: 137, 145–148; (2) Syriac Peshitta: 125–126, 145–148; (3) Vulgate: 111, 145–146; (4) Old Latin: 64.

5. Haggai's Personality

Attempting a character sketch of Haggai is next to impossible. Not only are we removed from him by centuries, but our evidence is also very meager. We can only characterize him for the fleeting moment he stands on center stage. Yet even this glimpse is important. To recognize the flesh and blood realities of biblical characters is to allow their lives more relevancy for our own experience.

First, Haggai was a man with a single-minded commitment to one cause. It is safe to imagine that Haggai had many interests in life. But for the historical moment, August through December 520 B.C., Haggai is like a man possessed, totally committed to the temple's reconstruction. His commitment stems from his profound conviction that a reconstructed temple represents the beginning of a greater restoration for God's people. Without being manipulative, he drives home the necessity for action, honestly and openly sharing his convictions with his people.

Furthermore, Haggai was a man of urgency. Current international turmoil was a sign to the prophet. God was at work in human history. The golden age of the future was imminent. God's dwelling in Jerusalem must be prepared for His coming. With a sense of urgency, Haggai inspired enthusiasm in the people, and they rebuilt the temple.

Finally, Haggai considered himself to be an instrument in God's hand. Here is the most striking characteristic of all. Over and over in this brief book we are told that this is "the word of Yahweh." That expression and others like it occur twenty-six times in the book's thirty-eight verses. Haggai's humility, his faithful submission to God's authority, and his servant role are clearly defined by his constant declaration, "Yahweh says."

Some commentators have demeaned Haggai, saying that his life and ministry offer us little today. But surely that is not the last word. Since God gauges us by faithfulness, will not the final word for Haggai be the divine declaration: "Well done, good and faithful servant" (Matt. 25:21)?

B. Haggai the Book

The Book of Haggai is the tenth in the minor prophet collection in the Hebrew Bible as well as in the ancient versions. It serves as one of the important historical sources for the post-exilic period. In all the Old Testament only Obadiah is shorter.

1. The Purpose of the Book of Haggai

Haggai's immediate purpose was to arouse his people from spiritual lethargy. He desired to see their faith put into practice in rebuilding the temple. But his concern was not merely for the physical structure. His proclamation contained far-reaching implications. The temple reconstruction was part of a larger picture that included God's final judgment of the nations, the advent of the the future golden age, and the reestablishment of the Davidic kingdom. Thus Haggai's purpose was eschatological as well as immediate and practical.

2. The Nature of the Literature in Haggai

To say that Haggai's literary skill has been disparaged by modern writers is a strong understatement. His work has been called "lifeless," "colorless," "featureless," "simple," "tame," and "unadorned." He has been accused of lacking imagination and brilliance. Unlike much of the Old Testament prophetic material, his book has usually been identified as prose rather than poetry.

The criticisms are unjust. Haggai's message is clear, uncompromising, and effective. Furthermore, scholars now recognize elements of poetry in the book. Parallelism, which was recognized earlier as a major characteristic of prophetic poetry, is present in 1:6 and 1:10. A refrain is found in 1:5 and 1:7, and a rhythmic effect is felt in 1:9–11 and 2:4–5.

A look at the book's structure puts the issue in proper perspective. Haggai combines prophetic sermons (or sermon summaries) and historical narratives.[2] While the historical narratives are prose, the sermons reflect poetic traces. More of a

---

[2]Consider Haggai 1, which contains historical narrative (1:1, 3, 12–15) and sermonic material (1:2, 4–11).

164 NAHUM, HABAKKUK, ZEPHANIAH, HAGGAI

poetic flair may have been present when Haggai actually preached these messages; this dimension may have been modified when the sermons were put into writing. Consequently while it is safe to conclude that Haggai uses a poetic style similar to the other prophets, it is impossible to demonstrate more than random poetic elements in the text as it now stands.

Stylistic features of the book include: (1) repetition (see 1:4 and 1:9; 1:5 and 1:7; 2:4; 2:6 and 2:21; 2:15 and 2:18); (2) lists (1:6, 11; 2:12, 19); and (3) interrogations (1:4, 9; 2:3, 12, 13, 19). Also the themes of judgment and blessing alternate effectively in the book's four sermons.[3] The various stylistic features add a dramatic effect to reading Haggai.

3. Critical Problems in the Book of Haggai

The book is assumed to contain abstracts or summaries of Haggai's messages. Add to this assumption the fact that the prophet is always referred to in the third person, and you have grounds for the question: Is Haggai the author of the book that bears his name? Most commentators think not, contending instead that a colleague or disciple or circle of disciples summarized Haggai's messages, prepared the historical narrative framework, and structured the book in its final form.

Though this scenario is possible, no evidence exists to deny authorship to Haggai himself. Surely Haggai could have summarized his own messages. Likewise nothing demands that a writer speak of himself in the first person. While the book is brief and probably not a record of all his preaching, no valid reasons exist for denying Haggai authorship.

Those who insist on the creative role of Haggai's unknown disciple nonetheless generally believe that Haggai wrote the sermons. Not surprisingly, a few scholars move beyond this view and deny Haggai wrote certain sermons. Most often called into question are the messages in 2:10–19 and 2:20–23. These extreme views have found little favor; they are based on weak and insufficient arguments.

---

[3]Sermons 1 and 3 (1:1–11; 2:10–19) tell of judgment—though judgment moves into blessing in sermon 3; sermons 2 and 4 (2:1–9; 2:20–23) tell of blessing.

Another critical problem is the quality of the Hebrew text. Some critical analyses of the book lead one to the conclusion that the text is beyond repair. Though there are some problems, the situation is not as bleak as some commentators would have us believe. In fact the Hebrew text is well-preserved and sound. Some differences are present with the LXX, for example, but this does not necessarily mean the Hebrew text is inaccurate. Sometimes the LXX translators made mistakes. The received Hebrew text differs little from the Haggai text found at Murabba'at. The latter is the oldest extant Hebrew manuscript of Haggai thus far discovered.

Perhaps the most difficult critical issue facing the interpreter of Haggai is the textual location of 2:10–19. Is this passage (or part of it) dislocated in the present text? Some commentators suggest that 2:10–14 and 2:15–19 constitute two separate sermons, fused together here without a genuine relationship to each other. Furthermore, the reference to the laying of the temple foundation in 2:18 seems out of place; the work on the temple had begun in 1:12–15 and was well under way in 2:1–9. The solution to these problems, some scholars say, is to move 2:15–19 to follow 1:15; the date in 2:18 is then changed to match that in 1:15.

The interpretation of 2:10–19 is most difficult. Yet, as will be shown later, the passage is open to meaningful interpretation as it stands. Furthermore, by rearranging the text, exegetes open the door to a rather unhappy interpretation.[4] It is far better to accept the canonical arrangement of the text. This decision is enhanced by a comparison with the Murabba'at manuscript. Though it is missing verse 11, its order is the same as that in the received text.

4. Major Theological Themes in the Book of Haggai

It is fashionable to characterize post-exilic prophecy as inferior to pre-exilic prophecy. Such criticism can be given more

---

[4]As the passage now stands, the "people" in 2:14 clearly refers to the Judean community. The removal of 2:15–19, however, leaves open their identity. Without the limits of the text to bind them, commentators arbitrarily identify the people as the Samaritans (though they are mentioned by name nowhere in the book). The verse then becomes a statement of rigid exclusiveness, making Haggai an advocate of a narrow, provincial Israel.

emphasis than it rightly deserves. Though Haggai is not an Isaiah or a Jeremiah, he carried out his calling from God as faithfully as they did. Without exaggerating his work, we can readily recognize the rich theological concepts undergirding his proclamation. His persistent call to the Judean community to rebuild the temple has unfortunately blinded some who have evaluated his work; they have seen his interest as purely ritual and consequently his theological worth as negligible. A summary of some theological themes in the book will perhaps put his practical concern for temple building in perspective.

First, Haggai believed that people can know the good life only in relationship with God. Such relationship is not possible until people are willing to come to Him with penitent hearts. Thus Haggai implores the people to "give careful thought to your ways" (see 1:5, 7), that is, evaluate your relationship with God and see your need for confession and repentance. They were then to build the temple as an act of faith. Building the temple in and of itself was not sufficient. Foundational to such outer action was the inner transformation.

When the people responded by beginning the building project, Haggai again emphasized the need for inner holiness. In a difficult passage (2:10–14), the prophet seems to say that the rebuilt sanctuary is in itself no guarantee of a genuine relationship with God. According to Haggai's larger theological outlook, the temple *must* be rebuilt; yet more is needed from the people than external action.

Second, Haggai believed that godlessness was directly connected to fruitlessness. The failure of the Judean community to live the life of faith and build the temple was the cause for the drought and disasters that plagued them (1:1–11). If the people would return to God, blessings would be theirs (2:10–19); in other words, godliness and fruitfulness are related.

Haggai's interpretation must not be put on an individual level. No one should use his book as a proof text that the person who walks in faith will never experience drought. In a fallen world, committed followers of God often struggle while those far from Him have much.

Haggai is rather illustrating one of the fundamental truths of the biblical revelation: a mysterious connection exists between

God, humanity, and nature. When humanity is out of harmony with God, the effect is felt at every level of existence.

Genesis 3 reveals it well. Here humanity in sin experiences alienation at four levels: from oneself, from other human beings, from God, and from nature (see 3:7–8, 17). That ultimate truth underlies Haggai's proclamation.

Third, Haggai believed an intimate relationship bound the temple to the golden age of the future. Is it too much to speculate that he had been influenced strongly by his predecessor Ezekiel? Ezekiel envisioned the new age replete with reconstructed temple and inexhaustible blessings (see Ezek. 40–48). To that temple the glory of God, which had departed for Jerusalem's judgment, would return (see Ezek. 9–11; 43:1–11). There He would remain with His people forever.

Added to the influence of Ezekiel's prophecies was the world situation in Haggai's day. The Persian Empire was in turmoil. Was this the prelude to that final world judgment that would usher in the golden age? If so, then it was imperative that the temple be reconstructed immediately. The time for "last things" was at hand (see 1:2). As both Isaiah and Micah had predicted, the temple would play a unique role in the golden age; then the nations would stream there to learn God's ways (see Isa. 2:1–4; Mic. 4:1–4). Thus, for Haggai, the temple's reconstruction was an essential part of the larger unfolding of the future.

Haggai's purposes were both eschatological (promises of the golden age) as well as immediate and practical (repent, build the temple). Notice that the eschatological promises encouraged the people to finish rebuilding.[5] At the same time, the rebuilding was the necessary precondition for the eschaton (the glorious future envisioned by the Old Testament prophets) to come. Clearly Haggai's purposes were significantly intertwined. To separate them is to miss the book's theological point.

Fourth, Haggai believed that God's authoritative represen-

---

[5] In the initial work the people became discouraged because the structure was not as magnificent as they had dreamed (2:1–9). Haggai then promised that when the great eschatological day came, God would give the new temple a glory greater than that of the original. While the building project was necessary, God's action, not the people's action, would bring in the eschatological age and its blessings (see 2:6–9, 19, 21–23).

tative in the golden age would be from the house of David. The prophet was so certain of the immediacy of it all that he named the contemporary Judean governor Zerubbabel, who was indeed from David's line, as God's "signet ring" (2:23).

Though the time of the new age was delayed and Zerubbabel was not the ultimate Davidic ruler, are we justified in labeling Haggai as a dreamer who was wrong? Is it not more appropriate to recognize the prophet's profound hope in God (not in Zerubbabel) and his belief that God would work through the Davidic line? Is it not accurate to see Zerubbabel as a postexilic representative of the ongoing promise of a Davidic ruler, a promise that was indeed fulfilled several centuries after the prophet? Does not the reference to Zerubbabel in our Lord's genealogy (see Matt. 1:12) enhance the historical continuity of God's promises that passed from generation to generation until fulfillment came? Perhaps a lesson for us in Haggai's prediction of Zerubbabel is that we should have the same intensity and urgency about the Second Coming of the Davidic ruler as Haggai had for His first coming!

Chapter 11

The Sermon of Rebuke
(Haggai 1:1–15)

Answers to certain probing questions clearly reveal a person's priorities. What, for example, occupies one's time? What dominates one's thoughts? Where does one invest energy and effort?

The priorities of post-exilic Judah were clearly recognizable. Time was spent in planting and building homes. In a time of economic distress, finances dominated thought. Energy was invested in worldly well-being.

Tragically the One who was to be the ultimate priority was sorely neglected. The temple, which symbolized God's presence, was in ruins. The people were content to let it remain that way. Declaring the time was not right for temple reconstruction, they rationalized their attitude and actions.

Adopting the judgmental speech so familiar to pre-exilic prophets, Haggai challenges his fellow citizens to examine their situation, to consider why they were struggling, and to recommit themselves to God and the reconstruction of His dwelling.

The chapter divides into three parts: (A) The Introduction to the Sermon (1:1); (B) The Body of the Sermon (1:2–11); and (C) The Response to the Sermon (1:12–15).

A. The Introduction to the Sermon (1:1)

Formal titles appear in most Old Testament prophetic books. Such is not the case with Haggai. The book begins with an introduction to the first prophetic message. It reveals the sermon's date, its source, and its recipients.

1. The Date of the Sermon (1:1a)

All of Haggai's recorded sermons fall in the second year of Darius the Great's reign, 520 B.C. While in exile the Judeans adopted the Babylonian calendar, which began in the spring. The sixth month, therefore, roughly corresponds to our present months of August and September. Based on a synchronization of calendars, the "first day of the sixth month" would be August 29.

The first day of each month was of special significance to the Judeans. It was the day of the new moon and as such was recognized as a holy day, often with ceremonies at the temple. Even the indifferent Judeans of Haggai's day may have observed the holy days, if for no other reason than to enjoy the festivities (see Ezra 3:5). One can well imagine that something was lacking when the services for this particular festival were conducted at the site of the ruined temple. Haggai's choice of days to deliver his first message surely was not accidental; he knew the emotions the people experienced on the festival day would aid him in his call for temple reconstruction. Furthermore, prophets were evidently expected to speak on the New Moon holy day (see 2 Kings 4:23).

2. The Source of the Sermon (1:1b)

Perhaps because a prophetic voice had not been heard in post-exilic days prior to Haggai, the prophet makes abundantly clear his role as God's messenger. The Hebrew literally reads: "The word of Yahweh was by the hand of Haggai the prophet." Yahweh is the message's sole source; Haggai is the voice to the people. The designation of Haggai as prophet amplifies the concept of instrumentality. Old Testament prophets spoke not for themselves but for God.

3. The Recipients of the Sermon (1:1c)

The message was directed initially to the two major figures in the post-exilic community, the civil and religious leaders. The people also were recipients, though this is clarified only in the verses that follow.

The political leader was Zerubbabel. His name means "seed of Babylon." Zerubbabel was a "seed of Babylon" only in the sense that he was born there; he was a Hebrew of Hebrews, one in whom his people placed great hope (see 2:23).

According to our text, Zerubbabel was Shealtiel's son and thus the grandson of Jehoiachin, the Judean king taken prisoner to Babylon in 597 B.C. (see 2 Kings 24:15). However, confusion exists about Zerubbabel's genealogical record. In 1 Chronicles 3:17–19 he is called the son of Pedaiah who was a younger brother of Shealtiel. He is also referred to as the grandson of Neri (David's descendant through his son Nathan) in Luke 3:27.

Unraveling the threads of this genealogy is rather difficult. One factor that may aid our effort is that the Hebrew word *bēn*, here rendered "son," has broad application. It can be translated "grandson" or even "descendant," making exact relationships sometimes difficult to determine.

Another consideration is that we may have here evidence of a levirate marriage. In ancient Israel when a husband died without children, one of his kinsmen married the widow and produced a child for the benefit of the deceased. Some commentators speculate that Pedaiah was the actual father of Zerubbabel, while the deceased Shealtiel was his legal father. Other scholars maintain that an adoption occurred somewhere in Zerubbabel's genealogical history (Shealtiel, for example, adopting Zerubbabel), thus allowing for the confusion in names and titles. Whatever the outcome of the genealogical investigation, Zerubbabel was a descendant of David, whether through Jehoiachin (and Solomon) or Neri (and Nathan).

The ecclesiastical head of the post-exilic community was Joshua (also spelled Jeshua), the high priest. He was the son of Jehozadak, who was taken prisoner to Babylon (1 Chron. 6:15), and the grandson of Seraiah (1 Chron. 6:14), high priest at the time of Jerusalem's fall. The latter was executed by the Babylonians (2 Kings 25:18–21; Jer. 52:24–27).

Joshua was born in Babylon and was among those who early returned to the Promised Land (see Ezra 2:1–2). His name means "Yahweh saves" or "Yahweh is salvation." Joshua and his forebears trace their roots to the family of Zadok, which was to be the chief priestly group in the restored temple (according to Ezekiel's earlier prophecy in Ezek. 40:46 and 44:4–16).

B. The Body of the Sermon (1:2–11)

Some writers believe that Haggai 1:2–11 summarizes several of Haggai's sermons, put together here as one message either by the prophet or an editor. Be that as it may, the passage demonstrates a clarity of theme and a unity of thought. The major issue is the Judean's spiritual indifference, which is the root cause of their disasters. Circumstances will not change unless they consider their ways and reverse their priorities.

1. The Issue of Priorities (1:2–4)

Haggai begins the sermon by again emphasizing his role as messenger. He brings to Zerubbabel and Joshua a word from God Himself. The name for God in verse 2 is "Yahweh of Hosts," rendered as "the LORD Almighty" in the NIV. This rather enigmatic phrase has been subjected to intensive research over the years. This research shows that "attempts to establish an adequate understanding of 'Yahweh of Hosts' are fraught with difficulty."[1]

Two obstacles illustrate the task's complexity. First, the title is used frequently in the Old Testament; it is found nearly 300 times in seventeen books.[2] Second, the title "enjoys a long history in the biblical tradition, ranging from its initial reference in the pre-monarchical era to post-exilic times."[3] The meaning, therefore, probably differs at various times in Old Testament history.

While some scholars have translated "Yahweh of Hosts" as "Yahweh of armies" and given it a military flavor, commentators generally recognize a broader application. The title probably refers to God as the Lord of all things, both on earth and in heaven, visible and invisible. The NIV has followed a rather recent view that sees the title as an intensive abstract plural, thus giving it the somewhat generalized translation "the LORD Almighty." This rendering seems to lose something of the richness of the word "hosts."

---

[1] Jay N. Boo Heflin, "An Exegetical and Theological Study of the Concept of the Heavenly Council in Ancient Israel" (Th.D. dissertation, Southwestern Baptist Theological Seminary, 1971), p. 169.

[2] The name is used fourteen times in Haggai.

[3] Heflin, "Heavenly Council," p. 169.

The Lord's word in verse 2 is a strong rebuke. The Judeans are referred to as "these people" (the Hebrew literally says "this people") rather than "my people" or some other such term that would designate their relationship with God. The phrase's tone is negative, indicating that their spiritual indifference has cut them off from God.

Their indifference is demonstrated by their failure to rebuild "the LORD's house."[4] They have rationalized their inaction by claiming "the time" was not right for such a project.

Why the Judeans reached this conclusion is not clear, though any number of reasons may have influenced them. Some commentators feel that perhaps since the times were hard, other matters needed to be settled before attention could be given to the temple. Others probably argued that unrest in the Persian Empire demanded a low profile for the moment. Still others perhaps added a "holy air" to their excuse-making. For example, a literalistic interpretation of Jeremiah's prophetic writings may have dictated their view. Had not Jeremiah said that the exile experience would last seventy years (Jer. 25:11–12; 29:10)? If Jerusalem had fallen in 587 B.C. and it was now only 520 B.C., were there not still three years of exile bitterness left? Perhaps when the three years had passed, the time would be opportune for building.

Regardless of these excuses, the basic issue was one of priority. The time would never be right for those who really did not care about the things of God. People have time for that which is important to them.

God's second strong rebuke in verse 4 shows that the people have been preoccupied with personal comfort. They had had ample time to build their own homes. All the while the temple—God's home—lay in ruins. What a striking contrast. What a revealing picture of selfishness.

---

[4]Haggai used the Hebrew word for "house" eight times in reference to the temple (1:2, 4, 8, 9, 14; 2:3, 7, 9), while he used the technical word for temple only twice (2:15, 18). This choice of terminology emphasizes his view that the temple was to be God's dwelling place. If the people refused to build God's house, they clearly demonstrated that they did not want Him in their midst. By rebuilding the temple, they would show their desire to make Him their ultimate priority. Haggai's terminology is another indication that his purpose far exceeded a mere building program.

It was evident where the Judean's hearts were. Their failure to rebuild the temple clearly identified their genuine priorities. They were more concerned about economic security than a relationship with God. His name could not even be found on their list of priorities. One wonders if Haggai did not perhaps remember with sadness that earlier word about the ultimate priority for this people: "You shall have no other gods before me" (Exod. 20:3).

2. The Futility of Wrong Priorities (1:5–6)

Their priorities thus confused, the Judeans experienced futility in their daily circumstances. The people did not seem to realize that God's presence meant prosperity and satisfaction, while His absence meant distress and death. They denied His presence by refusing to rebuild the temple. And according to Haggai this spiritual inaction produced the futility in their daily lives. The people's inability to understand what was happening illustrates well sin's capacity to blind people to reality.

In verse 6 Haggai vividly pictures the futility of the day. Though the people invested all their energy and effort into material well-being, their crops produced little. Supplies of food, water, and clothing did not meet the needs of the community. Economic conditions were so bad that wage earners hardly could purchase basic necessities before their money was gone.

Several interpreters suggest two negative dimensions in the prophet's vivid picture: (1) The people literally did not have enough of the basic necessities. (2) What they did have did not satisfy them because they were out of touch with the One who alone brings satisfaction to life.

For the Judeans these difficulties were simply another reason for spiritual indifference, but for Haggai that spiritual indifference created the difficulties. For him the spiritual problem simply manifested itself in physical terms. He saw but one solution: the people needed to consider their ways (1:5).[5] They needed to take stock of themselves, consider the attitudes

---

[5] The Hebrew literally reads: "Place your heart on your ways." Since the heart in Old Testament terminology can refer to the mind, emotions, and total being of a person, the prophet is calling for the people to do a thorough self-examination.

and actions that had led them to this moment, consider the consequences of those actions, and then respond accordingly. Though Haggai does not use the earlier prophetic call for repentance, it does not seem far afield to suggest it as his intention.

In that light, it is significant that he does not first call them to rebuild the temple. They must initially take care of the internal matter of right relationship with God; then they will be ready to take up the external service of temple building. But unless they take these steps and reorder their priorities, they will continue to experience futility.

3. The Reappraisal of Priorities (1:7–11)

Two themes previously mentioned are reiterated in the sermon's concluding section. First, Haggai exhorts the people to consider their ways (1:7). Second, he correlates their difficulties in daily living with their spiritual indifference (1:9–11).

Haggai amplifies the latter issue. For the first time, he makes it clear that their hardships are the result of God's displeasure and punitive action. The difficulties they contend with are expressions of divine judgment. God blows away what little they bring home from the field. He withholds the needed moisture, causing their crops to fail. It is His command to nature that has produced a devastating drought.

Why have these judgments occurred? The prophet's answer is clear. The people had feverishly attended to their own needs, to their own homes, while God's house remained "a ruin." Haggai's not so subtle implication is that a reversal of priorities would bring prosperity and blessing.[6] A major theological truth underlies this section: a person only knows the joys of living when he or she is in right relationship with God.

If the people are to change their present lot, they must take action. They must first consider their ways (1:7) and following

---

[6] Some people are concerned by Haggai's equations of spiritual commitment to material prosperity and spiritual indifference to material deprivation. Certainly we know the righteous sometimes suffer in a materialistic sense. One, therefore, should beware of oversimplification at this point. At the same time, Haggai's emphasis has validity and is well taken. There is a corollary between genuine prosperity and right relationship with God as well as a corollary between lack of real satisfaction and rejection of God.

that self-examination, they must demonstrate a new commitment to God by rebuilding the temple.

Haggai's instructions are pointed. The people are to "go up
into the mountains and bring down timber and build the house"
(1:8). Commentators differ about the mountains' location, some
opting for distant Lebanon with its costly cedars and others
opting for the hill-country around Jerusalem.

Notice that no call is made to gather stones, which were
surely needed for the reconstruction project. This omission is
glaring and was evidently for dramatic purpose. The people
knew they had to have stones—and there they were around
them in the rubble of earlier rebellion! The stones from the old
temple and the Jerusalem destroyed by divine judgment were
lying in heaps around the city, ready to be used. What greater
visual aid could Haggai have had for his message? What a
dramatic sermon in the omission of a call to gather stones!
Sometimes what is not said is as effective as what is said.

God indicates in verse 8 that the rebuilding of the temple
will give Him "pleasure" and that He will "be honored" in it.
The latter verb can be translated "I will be glorified." Commentators differ about this word's significance. Some contend it has
the nontheological emphasis suggested by the NIV translation.
Others point out that God's glory symbolizes His presence and
is of great theological import. Remember that Ezekiel had seen
God's glory depart from the temple to allow judgment to occur
(see Ezek. 9–11). That same prophet also predicted the return of
God's glory to the restored temple (see Ezek. 43:1–12). Is
Haggai here alluding to that significant event?

As we come to the sermon's close, the matter rests with the
Judean community. The people must now reappraise their
priorities. Will they heed Haggai's exhortation? Will they
consider their ways, renew their commitment to God, and begin
the building project? Or will they continue on the road of
futility? The choice belongs to them.

C. The Response to the Sermon (1:12–15)

People become sensitive to God's direction for their lives
when they are repentant and forgiven. Though verse 12 does not
refer to repentance in so many words, the concept is present in

the Judeans' response. The proclamation of the divine word led to a spiritual change in their lives. They are now obedient and reverent to the Lord "their God."[7]

In this light, note that the Judeans are here referred to as the "remnant." In the pre-exilic prophets, the remnant was the faithful nucleus of believers whom God would call forth out of judgment to be His unique people. The term is now applied to the post-exilic Judean community as they obey the prophetic word. Obedience is one aspect of faith. When people exhibit a genuine faith relationship with God they are called the "remnant." The same people who had once been called "this people" (see Hag. 1:2) are now called "the remnant."

Coupled with obedience is their fear of Yahweh. Fear in this context does not mean terror of Him and His judgment but rather reverential awe and respect for God as God. It demonstrates their proper attitude about their relationship toward Him and is yet another evidence of genuine change in their lives. Earlier they had been indifferent to Him. Now they have considered their ways, accepted responsibility for their sins, and turned to Him in obedient and reverential commitment.

To encourage them in their faithful response, Haggai shares a brief but profound word of encouragement: "I am with you" (1:13). This sentence translates only two Hebrew words, but how full of comfort they are. In the midst of the obstacles to their faith, God offers His presence, protection, and blessing. What could be more assuring than this promise! It is literally the promise of Immanuel.[8]

That the people's initial response was spiritual in nature is further confirmed by verse 14. Here Haggai succinctly states that God "stirred up" the spirits of the leaders and people alike. Their lives were characterized by spiritual change. Repentance had issued forth in faithful obedience and reverential fear.

This spiritual renewal was followed by the practical expression of genuine faith. They realized that God had wanted them to rebuild the temple from the outset. But earlier, when they

---

[7] The phrase "their God" (used three times in this section) indicates an existing right relationship between the Judeans and Yahweh. It is additional evidence to the spiritual renewal that had occurred.

[8] Immanuel means "God is with us."

were spiritually indifferent, they had not been sensitive to God's direction. Now they "began to work on the house of the LORD" (1:14). Their initial labor probably involved such things as clearing the temple site of debris, gathering the necessary materials for the project, and cleaning and reshaping the available stone.

The date of their practical beginning was "the twenty-fourth day of the sixth month" (1:15), or September 21, 520 B.C. Less than a month had passed since Haggai's initial sermon! Spiritual renewal had issued forth in practical action. Certainly this prophet accomplished more in a moment than many accomplish in a lifetime.

Chapter 12

The Sermons of Encouragement
(Haggai 2:1–23)

The remnant community had responded enthusiastically to Haggai's first sermon. Commencement of work on the temple reconstruction project followed spiritual renewal. But mountain-top experiences seem to be followed by a return to the valley of reality. Less than a month after the work started, enthusiasm waned. Discouragement overtook the laborers. They saw, from the work thus far completed, that the new structure would never compare favorably with the magnificent edifice built by Solomon. Furthermore, resources were limited and workers were few. Availability of gold and other such items of finery that adorned the earlier temple were obviously out of the question. Doubts began to plague the people. Was their effort worthwhile? Would they ever be able to complete the task? Such pessimism, at least in the minds of some, seems ever present in any great undertaking.

To meet the increasing gloom, Haggai preached three messages of hope and encouragement. Recorded in Haggai 2, the three sermons include: (A) The Glory of the New Temple (2:1–9); (B) The Blessing of the People (2:10–19); and (C) The Choice of Zerubbabel (2:20–23).

A. The Glory of the New Temple (2:1–9)

Haggai preached the first sermon in the trilogy of encouragement "on the twenty-first day of the seventh month" (2:1), or October 17, 520 B.C. This was the seventh day of the Feast of Tabernacles (or Booths), one of the three great annual festivals in ancient Israel. The feast had two major purposes. Historically it celebrated God's goodness to the Israelites during the days of wilderness-wandering. Agriculturally it celebrated the harvest just completed and thus was also called the Feast of Ingathering. During this festive occasion the people were released from their work to gather in Jerusalem to offer sacrifices and participate in other rituals.

But the feast in 520 B.C. must have been a sad affair. The harvest that year was of little consequence because the land was parched by drought (see Hag. 1:9–11). Though some work had been accomplished on the temple, it would obviously be a long time before the new structure was completed. Festival rituals would again have to be carried out in the ruined structure. Furthermore, there was a gnawing realization that the new temple would never be as splendid as the old one. As is to be expected in such circumstances, some people began to wallow in the past, making disparaging remarks about the initial efforts at reconstruction. This idealization of the past by the few old-timers who had seen Solomon's temple began to dampen the other workers' morale.

In the light of the intensifying despair, God spoke again through Haggai to Zerubbabel, Joshua, and the people at large (2:1–2). The community needed hope and encouragement if the work was to continue. Haggai intended to frame that hope in past, present, and future terms.

The prophet first raises a series of rhetorical questions designed to acknowledge the growing doubts of the people: "Who of you is left who saw this house in its former glory? How does it look to you now? Does it not seem to you like nothing?" (2:3).

The questions were not asked to discourage them further or to demean their concerns. Haggai recognized the obvious limitations of the day. In terms of material splendor and appearance, the new temple would not compare with the old. At the same time, Haggai wanted the people to realize that human estimations and divine appraisals were not the same. God's evaluation of the new temple was decidedly different from theirs. With that in mind he wanted them to claim the earlier promise (see Hag. 1:13) that God was with them and that His presence would make the difference. He was sufficient to overcome every obstacle at hand.

To emphasize the divine presence, Haggai reminded them of that great past action when God entered into covenant with Israel at the time of the Exodus (2:5). As God had been uniquely with the people then, so He had remained with them through the years. He reminded them: "And my Spirit remains among you" (2:5). Furthermore, He was still with them (2:4).

The awareness of God's continuing presence was to encourage the people. Because He was with them, their difficulties could be surmounted. Accordingly, they were to "be strong" (2:4). They were to "work" (2:4) and "not fear" (2:5). Since fear is diametrically opposed to faith, Haggai was calling them to reaffirm their faith relationship with God even as they continued to labor on the temple reconstruction project.

In verses 6–9 the prophet turns to future hope. He envisions a brief interval of history ("in a little while") and then the eschaton will commence with a cosmic upheaval ("I will once more shake . . ."). The judgment from God will create both natural ("I will . . . shake the heavens and the earth, the sea and the dry land") and political repercussions ("I will shake all nations"). In this judgmental shaking, "the desired of all nations will come" to the Jerusalem temple.

The identity of "the desired" has been vigorously debated. These words comprise perhaps the most difficult issue in the book's interpretation. The early position of Jewish rabbinical scholars was that the phrase was a personal reference to the Messiah. This position was adopted by Jerome in his translation of the Latin Vulgate, by Martin Luther, and by countless others. Luke 2:22–26 was considered to be the fulfillment of Haggai's prophecy.

But the majority of commentators today do not accept the messianic interpretation. Two major arguments oppose it.[1] The first is grammatical. The Hebrew verb "will come" is not singular, as we would expect if a person were the subject. The

---

[1] Another factor against the messianic interpretation is that the phrase "the desired" or "the desire" (KJV) is never used as a title or name for Christ in the New Testament.

word "desired" is a feminine singular noun, but because of the plural verb, it is considered a collective.[2] We can translate accordingly: "The desired things of (or the objects desired by) the nations," which would refer to their material treasures. In the coming golden age, these items will be brought to the temple, filling it "with glory" (2:7) or wealth. These were words of genuine hope to a discouraged people who had little possibility of adding material splendor to the structure on which they labored.

The second argument against the messianic interpretation is contextual. Verse 8 affirms divine ownership of silver and gold. If "the desired" that comes to the temple is the Messiah, this statement has little purpose in the present context. But if "the desired" is the wealth of the nations, verse 8 plays a major role. The thought is this: the nations' gold and silver belong ultimately to God; it is, therefore, within His right to bring what He will to the temple.

The assumption that "the desired" is the material treasure of the nations raises another issue. Does verse 7 imply that the Gentile nations bring their treasures as offerings to Jerusalem? Is this an expression of genuine worship? Or does the larger context imply that God, as rightful owner, shakes the nations as the wind shakes a tree laden with fruit, causing the treasures to fall off and then to be returned to Jerusalem through an unspecified agency? The passage is not clear. If one takes the first implication, a universal note is sounded in Haggai that is similar to Isaiah 60:1–11. People from other nations will share with Israel in God's salvation. It just may be that Haggai is seeing here a positive Gentile role in the world to come.

Verse 9 is the key to this sermon. It is Haggai's prophetic promise that "the glory of this present house will be greater than the glory of the former house." Is Haggai speaking here only in material terms? Some commentators contend so, arguing that the new temple will be blessed by an abundance of wealth never before seen, for it will come not only from the Jewish nation but

---

[2]Actually the noun may have been a plural in the original text. Hebrew is a language of consonants. The vowels were added to the Hebrew Bible after New Testament times. We could easily make the word "desired" a plural form by a simple change in vowels without any alteration of the consonants in the text.

also from the Gentile world. Those who take this view suggest that the second major statement of the verse—"I will grant peace"—simply means that God will grant prosperity through the accumulation of wealth.

It seems better, however, to recognize a dual meaning for glory in this verse. While it does represent material splendor, it also represents God's presence. For Haggai, God's presence with the people is already a reality (see 1:13; 2:4–5); His presence will also pervade the future golden age. Because God will be there, peace or *shālôm* will be granted. This peace means more than material prosperity; it means wholeness of life, tranquility, and completeness.[3]

Haggai's sermon was designed not only to encourage the people but also to help them see the importance of the rebuilding project. For "the desired" to come to Jerusalem, for the golden age to begin, the temple had to be reconstructed.

Though some commentators still see "the desired" as the Messiah, Haggai's more significant messianic affirmation in this sermon is the promise of verse 9. In terms of historical development and a unified biblical theology, the ultimate fulfillment of the greater glory of "this house" comes in the ministry of Christ, who erects a living, spiritual temple.

Remember that "this house" has historical continuity regardless of the different forms at different times. Be it the temple constructed with stone and wood by Solomon, Zerubbabel, or Herod, or the living temple constructed by Christ, it is still "this house." And its greatest glory is in Christ.

Haggai did not see this; he was limited historically. His vision was of a future temple of stone and material splendor, glorified by God's presence; there both Jew and Gentile would come to worship, knowing together God's peace. Though Haggai was himself limited, his prophetic words nevertheless have eschatological and messianic implications far beyond his vision.

---

[3]The statement "I will grant" is an imperfect Hebrew verbal form, indicating that the giving of peace is never completed; it is given over and over again.

B. The Blessing of the People (2:10-19)

The major problem in this section is the time-orientation. Not only does Haggai speak on a specified day, but he also employs historical flashbacks as well as future projections. It is not always easy to determine where he stands chronologically. Accordingly, the chronology must be considered briefly before we examine the sermon's content.

1. The Sermon's Time-Orientation

The sermon was preached "on the twenty-fourth day of the ninth month" (2:10). In the four verses that follow, Haggai uses a question-and-answer session with the priests to remind the people of their past defilement (2:11-14). These verses contain a flashback to the time before the prophet's initial sermon and the people's repentant responses. Haggai continues the flashback in verses 15-17 by reminding them that their defilement created devastating agricultural conditions that affected their quality of life. But he encourages them to focus on the day they started the temple reconstruction project as the day when their lot changed (2:18-19a). His implication is that while they could not yet see the change, it was in fact a reality.

But now, on the very day he spoke, on the "twenty-fourth day of the ninth month," they were going to know God's blessing. It would be evident "from this day on" into the undefined hereafter (2:19b). Thus the message concludes with a victorious prediction of immediate and future divine blessing.

2. The Sermon's Content

The date of the sermon was "the twenty-fourth day of the ninth month" (2:10), or December 18, 520 B.C. Three months had elapsed since the temple project was begun (see 1:15), and it was a little more than two months since the first sermon of encouragement (see 2:1). No religious festival occurred on December 18, but the time of year was agriculturally significant. It was the season of rains which were so crucial for the next year's harvest.

Following divine instruction, Haggai sought the legal opinion of the priests on two matters (2:11). The first concerned the law of communicated holiness. If a man carried "consecrated meat" (the flesh of an animal killed for a sacrifice) in his garment, did the garment communicate, or transmit, holiness to other items he touched? The priestly answer was negative (2:12).

But the second question, dealing with the law of defilement, brought an affirmative response. Those defiled by contact with dead bodies defiled whatever they touched (2:13). In other words, defilement or impurity is much easier to communicate than holiness or purity.

It is not necessary or even profitable to try to force every aspect of Haggai's legal inquiry in our interpretation. His method here is parabolic, designed to emphasize one major point. He wanted to show that the people in their past defilements corrupted everything they touched. That he was indeed thinking of the past is verified by reading verse 14 as follows: "So it was with this people and this nation in my sight."[4] This translation is perfectly justifiable from the Hebrew perspective.

Haggai does not say what past sin defiled them.[5] But since this section is a flashback, repetition is not necessary. The larger context of the book (see 1:1–11) clearly indicates that they were defiled by their spiritual indifference to God and the consequent failure to rebuild the temple. They had, in turn, communi-

---

[4]The attempt by some interpreters to identify "this people" in verse 14 as the Samaritans is without justification. It introduces a new element to the book that is nowhere else present and thereby smacks of eisegesis rather than exegesis. (Eisegesis is the practice of reading one's own views into Scripture. Exegesis is the work of interpreting and understanding what the Scripture itself says.) The phrase "this people" had earlier been used for the Judeans (see Hag. 1:2). Why would Haggai suddenly change subjects with no warning? Why should we bring the Samaritans into the picture when Haggai does not specifically do so?

[5]Some commentators contend that Haggai is speaking of present sin and defilement on the part of the people. God's people never do live up to His ideal and constantly need prodding. However, if the present passage is interpreted as new alienation from God during the time they have been working on the temple (in other words, they have reverted to the status of "this people"), it leaves no room for their confession and repentance that would then issue forth in the blessing that is pronounced in verse 19. While all of God's blessings to humanity are certainly signs of unmerited favor, positive human choice is still necessary (see Isa. 1:19–20). Thus this passage reflects alienated, sinful Judah before the people's response on September 21 (see Hag. 1:12–15) and not a newly fallen Judah on December 18.

cated their uncleanness to their crops. Thus the offerings they presented to the Lord were "defiled" (2:14). In verses 15–17 Haggai continues the historical flashback. He admonishes the people to consider their circumstances before they started the temple reconstruction project. His illustrations reiterate the theme of chapter 1:6 and 1:9–11. Because their crops were defiled by their uncleanness, the yield was always less than expected or needed. The supply of both grain products and wine was much less than the demand. Again Haggai explains that these past agricultural failures were God's punishment for their rebellion.

With verse 18 Haggai moves from the negative past to the positive present and future. From the very day on which he speaks (December 18), they are to "give careful thought to the day when the foundation of the LORD's temple was laid." That day three months earlier, when they had begun the temple restoration, was the turning point. From that very moment, with a restored relationship with God, they could expect circumstances to change.

Haggai's rhetorical question at the outset of verse 19 sets the stage for his victorious conclusion. The seed was not in the barn. It had been planted. It was too early for the crops to have begun to grow. But the rains were now in process. The time of growing had begun. Four months later the grain harvest would begin and shortly thereafter the harvest of the vineyards.

For Haggai, the next harvest seasons would reflect the new relationship with God. In joyous song the prophet, speaking for God, declares: "From this day on I will bless you." Past agricultural failures will give way to an abundance in harvest. The crops of the new year will reflect God's blessing on His repentant people.

C. The Choice of Zerubbabel (2:20–23)

Haggai's final sermon, like the one preceding, was preached December 18 (2:20). In it he presents a remarkable picture of the messianic era, with Zerubbabel standing in the unique role of God's representative. If the preceding sermon demonstrated that evil is more infectious than good (see especially 2:11–13), this final message shows that good is ultimately more powerful than evil. The pagan nations will be destroyed, and God's universal sovereignty will be established. This sermon is similar in several ways to the one preached on October 17 (2:1–9). In the earlier message, Haggai described a cosmic upheaval that in turn was to be followed by the eschaton; in the eschaton the new temple in Jerusalem would be glorified by the Gentiles bringing their offerings in worship.

Here Haggai again describes cosmic upheaval and the eschaton, but his concern is with Zerubbabel's messianic role. The imminence of the coming of God's kingdom in the sermon of October 17 (see the phrase "in a little while" in 2:6) becomes more evident in this final sermon. Haggai's identification of Zerubbabel as the messianic ruler underscores the imminence of these events in the prophet's mind.

This final sermon is specifically addressed to Zerubbabel (2:21). Though some commentators consider it to have been personal and private, this need not be the case. In fact, such a word to Zerubbabel would have been profoundly encouraging to the people.

To understand what these statements would mean to the people, consider these historical facts. In Jeremiah's day, the Davidic dynasty had lost its power. Not only was its kingdom brought to an abrupt close by the disastrous events of 587 B.C., but even more catastrophic had been Jeremiah's curse on the pre-exilic Davidic ruler Jehoiachin: "'As surely as I live,' declares the LORD, 'even if you, Jehoiachin, son of Jehoiakim king of Judah, were a signet ring on my right hand, I would still pull you off'" (Jer. 22:24). And further: "Record this man as if childless, a man who will not prosper in his lifetime, for none of his offspring will prosper, none will sit on the throne of David or rule anymore in Judah" (Jer. 22:30).

For many people, the intense hope focused in the Davidic dynasty had ended with Jeremiah's words. But now Haggai uses Jeremiah's language to reverse the earlier curse. The Davidic promises lost with Jehoiachin are renewed in Zerubbabel. To many Judeans, Haggai's word lifted hopes and produced a buoyant confidence.

The cosmic upheaval of the second sermon is expanded here, particularly in terms of impending social and political convulsions. Earlier Haggai declared: "I will shake all nations" (2:7). Now the expanded detail reveals that both the thrones of the pagan nations (representative of their political structures) as well as their military enterprise will be shattered even as God allows them to destroy each other (2:22). This last point underscores the key feature of verse 22: God is the world's absolute sovereign; before Him and through His means "the power" of the nations is shattered. Notice the repetition of the definitive statement "I will" throughout this final sermon.

Of monumental significance is the book's final verse (2:23). Here Haggai points to Zerubbabel's unique status in the eschaton. Haggai uses four specific ideas to illustrate Zerubbabel's role:

(1) "I will take you." This phraseology is used frequently in the Old Testament to describe a person selected by God for a vital responsibility.

(2) Zerubbabel is called God's "servant," a title used for many of the Old Testament heroes, including the patriarchs, Moses, David, and Job. The term has special significance in Isaiah 40–55.

(3) "I will make you like my signet ring." In the ancient world a signet ring was considered both the prized possession of the owner and the sign of his authority. It was always with him, worn either on his right hand (see Jer. 22:24) or on a cord around his neck (Gen. 38:18). The signet was used to stamp the owner's name or emblem on important documents. Thus Zerubbabel was to be not only Yahweh's prized possession but also His authoritative representative in the future kingdom.

(4) "I have chosen you" affirms divine selection; the verb often indicates that in which one takes pleasure. Note especially that these magnificent promises are contained in a verse that three times declares these are Yahweh's words!

To say the least, Haggai's identification of Zerubbabel as the messianic figure of the future golden age is bold, but it must not be misunderstood. To declare bluntly that Haggai was "wrong," as some interpreters do, is to miss several key points.

First, we see in the prophet's emphasis on the imminence of the eschaton the same kind of urgency which characterizes New Testament writers who eagerly anticipated the immediate

Second Coming of Christ. This kind of expectancy is part of a bold and vital faith. Perhaps Haggai should serve as an example to us all.

Second, Old Testament promises were occasionally given in the person of one figure, only to be ultimately fulfilled in another. Consider Abraham's call-experience in Genesis 12 as an example. To the patriarch God said: "All peoples on earth will be blessed through you" (12:3). Though that promise was to some degree realized in Abraham personally, it was ultimately fulfilled in One who came after Abraham. So it was with Haggai's promise to Zerubbabel.

Third, the fulfillment of Haggai 2:23 came not so much in Zerubbabel as a person but in the office he held. He was the new Davidic ruler. As such he was another historical link in the chain that led from David to the One who fulfilled the Davidic hopes.

Certainly Haggai's words are valid. Zerubbabel as a Davidic ruler *was* the chosen servant, the signet ring of God, the one selected for vital leadership. But in God's larger plan a greater One was yet to come to David's throne (see Luke 1:32). In Him the eschaton truly begins. He is the One who "will reign over the house of Jacob forever; his kingdom will never end" (Luke 1:33).

For Further Study on Haggai

1. In a Bible dictionary, read about Israel's exilic and early restoration periods (587–500 B.C.).

2. Joseph Parker was one of England's forceful biblical expositors in the preceding century. Read his articulate exposition of Haggai in *The People's Bible*. (Joseph Parker. *The People's Bible: Discourses Upon Holy Scripture*. New York: Funk & Wagnalls Co., 1982. 358–74.

3. Reread Haggai 1:4 and evaluate your personal priorities in light of this passage.

4. Read an article about the "Feast of Tabernacles" (or "Booths") in a Bible dictionary.

5. In the discussion of Haggai 2:9, I talked about the living temple constructed by Christ. Examine the following passages: John 2:19–21; 14:23; 2 Corinthians 6:16; Ephesians 2:19–22;

1 Peter 2:4–10. What insights do they give you about the living temple?

6. Read the excellent sermon on Haggai 1:6 found in *Maclaren's Expositions of Holy Scripture* (William B. Eerdman's Publishing Company). It examines "the realities of a godless life" and is entitled "Vain Toil."